Charles Fox Gardiner, Gilbert McClurg

The Colorado Springs Region as a Health Resort

Charles Fox Gardiner, Gilbert McClurg

The Colorado Springs Region as a Health Resort

ISBN/EAN: 9783742860828

Manufactured in Europe, USA, Canada, Australia, Japa

Cover: Foto ©Thomas Meinert / pixelio.de

Manufactured and distributed by brebook publishing software
(www.brebook.com)

Charles Fox Gardiner, Gilbert McClurg

The Colorado Springs Region as a Health Resort

....The....

Colorado Springs Region

AS A HEALTH RESORT:

High Altitudes for Invalids.

❧

Compiled by
CHARLES FOX GARDINER, M. D., and
GILBERT McCLURG, Secretary
of the
Colorado Springs Chamber of Commerce.

❧

Published by the
Chamber of Commerce, Colorado Springs,
1898.

Preface.

By means of the able series of essays contributed by the skilled collaborators in this pamphlet, I am able to present to the medical profession an array of facts and statistics relating to Colorado Springs and the surrounding region, which is as accurate as diversified.

Medical science, as specially applied to the needs of the classes of invalids who are likely to become sojourners or residents in our midst; scientific dissertations upon climatology of high altitudes; tabular statements regarding water supply and mineral springs; general information relating to hygiene and sanitation, business and social aspects of Colorado Springs;—will be found embodied in the various treatises of "The Colorado Springs Region as a Health Resort: High Altitude for Invalids,"—each bearing the seal of authoritative fact from a recognized specialist.

Therefore, nothing remains for the compiler to add, save his thanks to those who have, by their knowledge and hearty co-operation, rendered such a publication possible,* —and a commendation of its contents, not only to physicians, but to the intelligent, reading-public, who as laymen (like the present writer) are practically cognizant of the advantages of this unrivaled Sanatorium, and who will rejoice to see its benefits and attractions stamped with scientific analysis and approval.

GILBERT McCLURG,

*Thanks are due in particular for the editorial work of Chas Fox Gardiner, M, D., of Colorado Springs, Chairman of the Executive Committee of The El Paso County Medical Society, of Colorado.

All inquiries concerning Colorado Springs and the Pike's Peak region will receive full and prompt replies if addressed to GILBERT McCLURG,

Secretary Chamber of Commerce, Colorado Springs, Colorado.

Table of Contents.

From "Lessons from an Old Master."

What is the help that cometh from the hills?
Strong pulses, full-drawn breath, and sinews tried?
Still may they cleanse the body of its ills;
But higher virtues have the hills supplied:
They train the soul to climb ; they best provide
The health of spirit, sanity of mind,
Wherein the purest fires of life reside,
And noble souls of old were quick to find
God in the wilderness and on the mountain shrined.

—ERNEST WHITNEY.

※

Colorado Springs.

City of Sunshine ! in whose gates of light
Celestial airs and essences abound ;
City of Refuge ! from whose sacred height
Disease falls thwarted as a baffled hound,
Loosing its fang, long burning in the wound;
City of Life ! thou hast a gift of years
For all ; swift Death a thousand times discrowned
Within thy walls, and Fate, with waiting shears,
Heed thee, as thou alone of earth didst feed their fears.

—ERNEST WHITNEY.

Colorado—About its Climate.

By J. C. Dana and Carroll E. Edson, M. D., of Denver, Colo.

THE STATE IN OUTLINE.

Colorado's area is over 100,000 square miles, nearly twice that of all New England. Of this great region, the eastern part, one-third of the entire state, is a rolling plain, the eastern border of which is 3,500 feet, and the western, where it touches the foot hills, 4,000 to 6,000 feet above sea level. The mountain system which covers the western two-thirds of the state is too complex to admit of brief description. It is enough here to say that behind the high ramparts of the Front Range, four great parks or valleys or mountain basins stretch north and south across the state, with an elevation, as to their rolling or level floors, of from 7,000 to 9,000 feet, and that between these and the state's western boundary are many mountain ranges and isolated peaks rising out of wide plateaus. In and out of this 60,000 square miles of mountain, park and table land, flow the Arkansas, the Platte, the Dolores, the Grand, the Bear and other rivers. Along these rivers and their tributaries are thousands of miles of valleys, some of them narrow canons and little more, many of them broad, fertile and inviting. These valleys vary in elevation from 4,000 feet to 8,000 or 9,000 feet.

Colorado climate is, of course, as varied, in many of its aspects, as is the surface of the state itself. On the mountain peaks, 14,000 feet above the sea, is perpetual snow, with scant Alpine vegetation peeping forth at summer beside the drifts. In the lower valleys the climate is almost semi-tropical, and here delicious peaches, grapes and similar fruits are easily and profitably grown. Between these two extremes are found climates of all degrees of temperature. Places at same altitude, moreover, in different parts of the state, varying as to the trend of the valleys in which they lie and as to their exposure to the winds, vary also, and widely, as to their temperature and their attractiveness as places of residence.

Three things common to all Colorado, however, must never be lost sight of—blue sky, sunshine and dry air. All over the state it is true that, save in the highest altitudes—say above 7,000 feet—on most days through midwinter, it is possible for one to sit in comfort in the sunshine in any sheltered nook. It is this almost perpetual sunshine which has perhaps more to do with the exhilarating effect of Colorado's climate on both well and sick than any other one factor.

WHY THE CLIMATE MAKES FRIENDS.

The Coloradoan visits his old home in Iowa or Ohio, or Pennsylvania, or New England, or in the South, for a few weeks and returns to his adopted home, and "Did you have a pleasant time?" is the first question that greets him. And over and over again comes the answer, "O, yes; except for the weather. It was so damp and oppressive—or cold and cloudy all the time."

The climate of America as a whole is brilliant and sunshiny, relatively, to that of much of the world; but the climate of the eastern states, when compared with that of Colorado, is so cloudy and damp and depressing that one who has lived here for a year or two feels most deeply when he returns there ·the lack of blue sky and cheering sun.

The new life in the new country; the swift passing of events; the possibilities of advancement and of fortune; the stir incident to the beginnings of things; all these are attractive to many, and go far to compensate for the loss of old friends and for the breaking of home ties and for that shifting of the scene of one's life which is a hardship to most. But over and above all the attractions of the newness and swiftness of western things is the attraction of the climate of our state; and many who have come to Colorado for other reasons have been led to stay, because they felt that here, under our sun and the inspiration of our sparkling dry air, their life would be happier and fuller and more satisfactory than it could be under the too often clouded skies of the East or South.,

THE SUNSHINE.

The sun in Colorado—in that great tract along and among the eastern foothills, in which are located Denver, Colorado Springs, Manitou, Pueblo, Trinidad, Golden, Boulder, Fort Collins and Greeley; in that region to which the tourist and the invalid are most likely to come and in which they are likely to stay longest—the sun here shines about sixty-two hours out of every hundred in which it is above the horizon. In Philadelphia the ratio is forty-nine. During the winter months, the trying time for the invalid, the difference is more striking still. In Colorado we have from December to March, 56 per cent. of all possible sunshine. In Philadelphia they get but 37 per cent.; a difference in Colorado's favor of over one-half. In ten years there were in Denver, on the average in each year, 314 clear or partly clear days.

(P. E. Doudna, Observer at Colorado Springs, reports but 57 cloudy days as an average for ten years.—Editor.)

In Chicago, in the same period, there were only 251; in New York, 262. During the three winter months the sun shines four out of every five days. Nor do these figures tell the whole story. One of the greatest advantages of this eastern belt along the front of the range is the early morning sunshine. There are no high mountain ranges for the sun to climb, as in so many high altitude resorts in other lands, but its first rays above the low eastern horizon are at once warming and cheering. The sun is up before the invalid is awake, and the air is warmed for his outdoor life without a long wait till mid-morning. In Davos, Switzerland, the sun on January 1 does not rise till 10 a. m., and sets at 3 in the afternoon, a possible sunshine of only five hours. In Denver on January 1 the sun rises at half-past seven a. m. and does not set till after half-past four; more than nine hours of sunshine.

Neither do the cloudy days preclude an outdoor life, as might be inferred. They do not bring the damp and rawness of the eastern or middle states. To many there is a restfulness in a clouded day from the constant intensity of clear blue sky.

THE TEMPERATURE, ACTUAL AND FELT.

The dryness and the rarity of the air make the sun's direct rays hotter and seemingly more penetrating here than in lower altitudes. Colorado sunshine will dry the soil, soften the atmosphere, and warm up every one who steps into it after a winter's storm in far less time than will the sunshine which falls through the damp and heavy atmosphere of the East.

The dryness of the air of this great mid-continental table land, and the consequent rapidity of evaporation, must be kept in mind in considering Colorado's temperatures, would one gain an accurate understanding of the climate as one feels it. The average July temperature of Denver is 72.1 degrees. The sensible temperature of the same month, the temperature that is, reduced to eastern terms, is only 57 degrees. The Colorado summer corresponds as to the feelings of those who pass through it, to that of Manitoba, of the Thousand Islands, of the Adirondacks, or of the White Mountains. (Capt. Glassford.)

The summer heat is occasionally seemingly intense; but it is really little felt, causes very little inconvenience, and never any suffering. In the hottest of summer weather it is but a step from the heat of the sunshine into the shade, which is always cool. Sunstroke is here unknown.

The coolness in the shade in Colorado, due to the very rapid dissipation of heat by reason of the rarity of the air, is something often spoken of but not easily impressed sufficiently on those not familiar with it. It makes it possible for one to live with great comfort even during a summer when the general temperature, as shown by a thermometer exposed to the direct rays of the sun, would seem to be almost unbearable.

The mean annual temperature of Denver is 50 degrees.

(The mean annual temperature, reported at Colorado Springs, is 47 degrees.—Editor.)

The mean annual temperature of all the most thickly populated part of the state, just east of the mountains, is from 45 to 50 degrees.

Captain W. A. Glassford, chief signal officer, Department of Colorado, has contributed an article to the report for 1894 of the Colorado State Board of Health on the subject of the actual as compared with apparent climate, and from this article some of the points given above are taken. "When the published record," he says, "of the heat in Boston, New York, Washington, St. Louis and Chicago is above 100 degrees it is simply unbearable; while the same recorded temperature at Denver is attended with little discomfort. Why? Because in the East moisture is present to a very considerable extent in the atmosphere, while in the West it is almost absent."

Owing to this great dryness of the air, and its small capacity for holding heat, there is throughout the year a difference of from 40 to 60 degrees between the sun temperature and the air. It is this great difference which makes the summer air so cool and comfortable. And in the winter, when the air is cold and bracing, one has but to step across from the shade into the sunshine to find the great warmth of its rays, 40 degrees higher. In mid-winter it is not uncommon to see two thermometers on the same veranda, one standing at 30 degrees in the shade, and the other in the sun at 85 degrees.

The cold air in winter is not apparent nor piercing as in damp climates, but clear and bracing, stimulating to nutrition and mental activity.

SPRING, SUMMER, AUTUMN, WINTER.

Speaking again of that part of Colorado which is most inhabited and is best adapted to the wants of the pleasure seeker or the invalid, a strip of ten to fifty miles in width, where plains and mountains meet—the temperate belt, as Captain Glassford calls it— one may say of the seasons:

Spring.—In Colorado we escape March; that is, this month here is so much less a time of rain and snow and slush and mud and bitter winds, than it is in the East, that it passes without particular notice. During the month of March and in early April snowfalls are not uncommon; but they disappear very rapidly under the heat of the sun. In a few hours the snow has evaporated, there is no melting into slush or wet, and often twenty-four hours after one of these short snows the dust is blowing on the sunny side of the road. The rapid disappearance of the snow is as incomprehensible to one who has not seen it as it is astonishing to the beholder. The temperature in these months does not often fall below 30 degrees, and commonly before the end of March the warm sunshine has begun to bring out the grass and to swell the buds on the trees and to call back the birds. April is a growing month, and in May the plains and the country generally are at their greenest.

The mean minimum temperature for March for ten years at Denver was 27.6 degrees, and the mean maximum temperature for May was 68.9 degrees. The rainfall in the whole three months of Spring in Denver averages only about five inches.

Summer.—June and July are the hottest months—and by August the mean temperature begins to decrease. The mean maximum temperature for July is 86.3 degrees. The direct rays of the sun are very intense and hot, but the air is cool and dry, and consequently the heat is easily borne. It is rare to see moisture on the soda fountains, and there is the comfort of a dry skin and unwilted collars. At sunset the air at once cools rapidly and the nights are always comfortable. There are comparatively few nights in summer when one does not need a blanket covering before morning. It is common to have a heavy but short shower in the last of the afternoon or early evening during these months, especially near the mountains, but they are not an interruption to out-door life and serve to lay the dust of the sun-baked plains.

Autumn.—The Autumn in Colorado, as in many other regions, is the most delightful part of the year. From September to nearly Christmas there is an almost unbroken period of delicious, sparkling days. All over the state it is not uncommon to have, during these months, a period of six or even ten or twelve weeks with scarcely a cloud in the sky from day to day, a brilliant sun, and high winds only on very rare occasions. The ground is dry, the air—as the nights grow cool—is even more bracing than usual. In all respects this is in Colorado the ideal season for the invalid or the tourist.

The mean temperature of the air along the eastern foothills in Colorado (4,000 to 6,500 feet), taking Denver for example, for September is 63 degrees; for October, 51 degrees, and for November, 39 degrees.

At higher elevations in the mountains the nights get quite cool in September, and ice forms at eight or nine thousand feet not infrequently in October; but even in high altitudes storms or periods of extreme cold in these three months are infrequent.

Winter.—The fine weather of the Autumn months often continues to the middle of November, and occasionally as late as to the last of December. A noticeable thing about the climate of the winter months in Colorado is that if one lives for a few years at a high altitude, even as great as that of Leadville—about 10,000 feet—and then spends a winter or two among the foothills at an elevation of from five to six thousand feet, he does not notice any great difference in the temperature of the winter or in the number and severity of the storms. In every part of the state below 10,000 feet and above 4,000 feet, there are during each winter several periods of from three to ten days of cold weather, usually preceded by a snow storm, and perhaps accompanied by one or two days of considerable wind. But these periods of cold weather, even when on rare occasions the thermometer goes several degrees below zero, are not felt to anything like the extent that similar temperature is in a damp climate. And it probably is a fact that the physical sensations of a winter at eight or nine thousand feet or at five or six in Colorado are very similar, and that the covering needed, and the precautions naturally taken against cold are of about the same nature in both altitudes. This fact is mentioned to call attention again to the persistent characteristics of the climate—dryness and sunshine—of every part of the State.

The sun is more often clouded in the winter months than in the rest of the year; but it can not be too often stated that the winter's sun is warm and invigorating, and that there are few days in the whole season so disagreeable as to make it impossible for any ordinary invalid to remain out of doors.

There is no accumulation of snow along the eastern belt of country—Denver, Colorado Springs, etc. A few days or a week and all traces of it are gone save on the northern side of banks or sheltered places. And it disappears without melting into slush or icy pools; the dry wind licks it up into quick disappearing vapor. The snow does not house the invalid save while it is falling. There is no piling up of drifts to give a long damp melting time in spring.

Along the eastern foothills the average mid-day temperature of the air is 45.5 degrees for December, 27.3 degrees for January, and 48.0 degrees for February. The total rainfall in Denver for these three months in 1892 was 2.47 inches.

(In Colorado Springs the bicyclist may ride his wheel every day in the year.—Editor.)

The open street cars are run all winter.

The clothing worn in Colorado, save high in the mountains, is such as is commonly worn in New York and New England and in the western states of about the same latitude, except that in winter the heavy overcoat is less needed, and in summer the thinnest underwear is apt to prove not quite heavy enough.

COLORADO AS A RESORT FOR INVALIDS.

Abundant sunshine, an invigorating, dry, sterile air; elevation above sea level and unrivalled opportunity for out-door life, are the great advantages which Colorado offers for the restoration of the consumptive's health. They are the prime factors in all such cures.

Three facts are now well established:

First—That pulmonary tuberculosis is a curable disease.

Second—Other conditions being equal, the completeness of the cure depends on the promptness with which the patient is put in proper surroundings.

Third—That of all aids yet found for the cure of this disease, suitable climatic surroundings are the most efficient.

The consensus of the best medical authorities is unanimous that out-door life amid sunshine and dry air, at a high elevation, assures the best results.

"The most notable advance in the treatment of consumption achieved during the present century has unquestionably been the rapid progress in public and professional favor of the High Altitude sanatoria." (J. A. Lindsay, M. D.) As the same writer says, "The High Altitude treatment of consumption is not a mere arbitrary innovation, but rests upon a solid substratum of fact, and its utility is explicable on lines of ascertained knowledge."

"I am as sure as I can be that recoveries from phthisis, judiciously treated at high altitudes, are much more numerous and much more lasting than those treated by any other method at any other place." (Sir Andrew Clark.)

"In selecting a climate for a consumptive, the first question which occurs to us is the inquiry as regards the proportion of pleasant, sunny days, in which out-door exercise can be safely enjoyed."

"The first desideratum is a large proportion of fine, sunny weather."

"In all such cases (consumption) there is one essential and predominating condition to be fulfilled, as we have already said, and that is the selection of a climate in which an out-door life in fresh, pure air, can be largely followed." (Burney Yeo, M. D.)

Dr. Herman Weber, in his classic lectures on pulmonary phthisis, says: "Pure air is the most important means of cure—food and an out-door life." Speaking of the advantages of high altitude in the cure of consumption, he says: "The main features of a mountain resort important to us are:

"I. The purity or aseptic nature of the air.

"II. Dryness of the air and soil.

"III. Coldness or coolness of the air and great warmth of the sun temperature.

"IV. Rarefaction and low pressure of the air.

"V. Intensity of light.

"VI. Stillness of the air in winter.

"VII. A large amount of ozone."

All of the factors are ideally present in Colorado's climate—elevation, from 4,000 feet to any desirable height; as dry and sterile an air as can be found; prolonged hours of intense, warm sunlight beneath an unclouded expanse of blue sky, and less annual wind movement than any of the large cities of the country.

Dr. Weber himself says, after speaking of European stations: "More important to us in the treatment of phthisis are the mountain resorts of North America. In the Rocky Mountains of the United States we possess indeed an endless variety of mountain climates."

"The effects on the invalid suited to such climates are increase of appetite, improvement of sanguification and general nutrition, strengthening of the heart and circulation, raising of muscular and nervous energy. Under the influence of such constitutional progress, which is assisted by the local action of aseptic, dry, cold air, by increased ventilation of the lungs, we observe a gradual improvement in the state of the lungs, leading not infrequently to arrest of the disease and actual cure." (Herman Weber, M. D.)

Dr. F. I. Knight, of Boston, says: "There seems little doubt that in suitable cases the improvement in nutritive activity is much more marked in mountainous regions than on the plains."

"The region which I have found the best for this kind of treatment is the eastern slope of the Rocky Mountains in the states of Colorado and New Mexico, where the altitude ranges from four thousand to eight thousand feet."

"I do not hesitate to say that the eastern slope of the American 'backbone' offers as good climatic conditions as the European resorts, or even better.'

"Colorado ought to be the sanatorium of the United States. I fully believe it has the stuff in it to merit this name." (Carl Ruedi, M. D.)

Dr. S. E. Solly, of Colorado Springs, by a careful analysis of 2,598 cases of pulmonary phthisis treated at various altitudes, shows that in high altitudes 76 per cent. of all cases improve as against 59 per cent. treated at sea level, while of cases in the early first stage 89 per cent. improve at high altitudes.

"This inquiry," he says, "has clearly demonstrated two things, viz.: That the majority of consumptives do better, other things being equal, the farther they are removed from the sea, and that they do better in high than in low altitudes."

"The final conclusion is that a consumptive treated in an open resort in an elevated climate has three times as good a chance of recovery as has one treated in an open resort in a low climate and twice as good a chance as one treated in a sanatorium in a low climate."

The figures and conclusions agree with those of Dr. S. A. Fisk, of Denver, who reports improvement in 67 per cent. of cases coming to Colorado, and marked improvement in 50 per cent., adding: "I think these figures might be somewhat increased in favor of the good influence of our climate if only all patients would act cautiously and with discretion, which, unfortunately, they will not."

"Taking cases as they come to us, we can expect improvement in two out of three; men do better than women, as they do anywhere; persons over twenty do better than those under, and those over thirty do still better."

Dr. S. G. Bonney, in a report of 200 cases, states "that of 40 cases with slight invasion, in the incipient stage, 90 per cent. received material benefit; of 54 cases of more marked involvement, consolidation, beginning cavity or infection of both lungs, 79 per cent. improved; of advanced cases 55 per cent. improved, a large proportion in view of the character of the cases.

"Of all cases 69 per cent. improved; 45 per cent. had marked improvement, and 16½ per cent. complete arrest."

While in general Colorado benefits most cases of consumption, its chief efficiency is in the early stages of slight invasion, before there is marked involvement of lung tissue or serious impairment of the general health. These are the cases which should be sent promptly to Colorado.

Colorado's beneficent climate should be the first and not a last resort.

Dr. F. I. Knight classes the cases most likely to do well here, as follows:

"I. Early apical affection.

"II. Patients with more advanced disease, some consolidation but no cavity or serious disturbance.

"III. Hemorrhagic cases; early cases with haemopticis and without much fever are benefited.

"IV. A small, quiet cavity is not a contra-indication.

"V. Cases of consolidation remaining after pneumonia or pleurisy, do well.

"VI. Laryngeal cases do no worse than anywhere else."

Unfortunately, as Dr. C. J. B. Williams says, "there are a certain number of cases where the best of climates avail nothing, namely, acute tuberculosis, laryngeal phthisis, advanced excavation, and cases with intestinal ulceration and albuminuria."

Cases of advanced and destructive lesions; those complicated with serious disease of the heart, or with marked emphysema; those who have a marked erethic constitution and who do not sleep or nourish well in high altitudes, and those with marked sepsis, do not do well and should not be sent here.

OTHER CONDITIONS OF INVALIDISM.

Cases of bronchial irritation, catarrhal states of the throat and air passages, are generally improved.

Many cases of asthma are permanently relieved.

Dr. J. N. Hall says, in the Colorado Climatologist: "There seems no reason for thinking that any functional derangement of the heart is unfavorably influenced by residence at this altitude."

And Dr. H. B. Whitney, in the same journal, says: "A moderately high altitude is not contra-indicated by any case of valvular disease where compensation has been constant and there are no present signs of threatened cardiac weakness."

And Dr. W. P. Munn, again in the same journal, says: "Only the functional cardiac trouble dependent upon extensive pulmonary involvement is aggravated at this altitude. Other persons having cardiac disease live as comfortably and as long in Colorado as in any other region. The percentage of deaths in Denver due to diseases of the heart and to that closely allied condition, Bright's disease, is shown by the records of the health department of that city to be very much smaller than the percentage due to those causes in any other city in the United States having a population exceeding 100,000. The same statement is true in regard to pneumonia and bronchitis. Irresponsible writers have imagined that these diseases ought to be more prevalent and fatal here than elsewhere, from belief to assertion has been but a short step, and their erroneous statements have been disseminated and have been largely accepted as correct, simply because they have not been contradicted."

Dr. J. T. Eskridge, in the Colorado Climatologist, says: "High altitudes, and more especially the altitudes of Colorado which are sought by invalids, afford no form of nervous or mental disease that is not common at sea level. Doctors have failed to detect any difference, attributable to altitude alone, in the causes, course, frequency and prognosis of organic disease of the nervous system between those observed in Colorado and affections of like nature treated at sea level."

The dry, clear air, without a trace of dampness, and the intense, warm sunshine, give a climate of great relief to many rheumatic cases.

MEDICAL SUPERVISION OF THE INVALID.

Too many invalids coming to Colorado depend upon their own ideas or the suggestions of their friends as to their conduct of life, often to their great detriment. Even physicians who have not lived here should not attempt to direct the patient in so new and different a climate.

"It would be better for the patient if he would exercise more wisdom and acknowledge his ignorance, and withhold advice altogether." (Anderson.)

"The benefit derived is dependent not upon climate alone, but as well upon conscientious attention to mode of life and management." (Bonney.)

"It is the duty of our profession," says Dr. Herman Weber, "to teach the public that it is a great mistake to think that the invalid and his friends are able to manage the dietic and hygienic treatment of consumption, or that it is enough to go for a season to a certain climatic health resort, and that the climate itself is able to cure phthisis, without the assistance of local doctors. Many valuable lives are lost through this error, even under the most favorable climatic circumstances, lives which might be saved under strict medical guidance."

Such is the unanimous and unmistakable verdict upon the advantages of elevated climate. Colorado fulfils all the conditions to a remarkable degree.

Resorts of every desirable elevation from 4,000 to 10,000 feet are within easy reach of large centers of population.

The soil and air are remarkably dry—there are but fourteen inches of rainfall in the year, and at some stations even less—no periods of prolonged cloudiness or rain.

Its average mean relative humidity is only 52 per cent., and its absolute moisture averages but 1.8 grains of vapor to the cubic foot.

Its temperature is cool and bracing, restoring the wasted energy and stimulating the nutrition, lending new zest and hopefulness.

Its sunshine is brilliant, penetrating and continued, with a higher average number of cloudless, sparkling days than any other climate.

Attractions to an out-door life are present on every hand, and the invalid is irresistibly drawn out into the pure, fresh air and dancing sunlight. The wide horizon, with its beauty of soft, level plain or grandeur of mountain peaks, is a constant joy, and the enforced quiet of recovery loses all its irksomeness.

"It is not contended that our climate is the be-all and cure-all but we know that the absence of endemic phthisis and a dry soil are strong arguments in favor of this being a curative climate. We know, further that an out-door life is possible during more hours of the day and during more days in the year than in almost any other climate on the face of the earth; but the most conclusive testimony to be found as regards the curative influence of a life in Colorado, is in the thousands upon thousands of people who have found recovery here and pitched their tents, and who can in their own persons bear testimony to the fact."

COLORADO IS A HOME, NOT MERELY A SANATORIUM.

The most fortunate and valuable feature of Colorado as a climatic station is that all its benefits and health-giving conditions are at hand and offered to the invalid without his going into exile to obtain them. He has not to seek a wilderness or a small sanatorium on some isolated Alp. More than any other factor should this fact appeal to the invalid. To recover his health in Colorado he does not need to exile himself from the comforts of his daily life or human intercourse. For the clear, pure air, which is so abundant, even the advantages of city life need not be foregone. To one with a family especially is it a rare privilege to find so easily a healthful out-door life in sunny fields, a mile above sea level, and yet give his children the advantages of schooling and civil education, libraries, opportunities for music and intellectual enjoyment.

Throughout the state the schools are all of the highest grade. With all the multiplied helps that a large city offers, there is always at hand the more varied attractions to a vigorous out-door life.

Colorado climate invites to outdoor life. There is no season of the year, and in fact there are few days in the year, in which one can not be out of doors with comparative comfort. This, added to the fact that the air is bracing and the sunshine inspiring, leads to a great deal of walking and driving and riding and bicycling and outdoor sports. The result of this on health is perhaps shown more clearly in the children of Colorado than in the adults. When one considers that a very large proportion of Colorado parents are people who came to the state as invalids, the healthy appearance of the children one meets on the streets and sees collected in school-rooms or at play on the athletic grounds is something remarkable. They are full-chested, strong-limbed and bronzed.

Surrounding such a city of rare freedom from foul, contaminated air, lies the open, generous beauty of the country, appealing ever to the invalid as his strength returns and offering him new attractions to an outdoor life; wide areas of country still little more than a wilderness in which to hunt, fish and explore; most admirable opportunities for geological study; a varied flora of great interest to the botanical student; an insect life unusually rich, attractive to the entomologist; and unsurpassed opportunities for the study of bird-life, there being a larger number of varieties of birds found within this state than in any other of the Union save one.

Within easy reach are wild, untracked areas, abounding in game of every sort, to tempt the rugged and strong; for the zest of the chase, the wild hunt of the bear, are not for the invalid's early days of the new Colorado life, but are a reward of patient, healthful waiting.

Not only does Colorado provide pleasant and helpful surroundings for the invalid during his convalescence, but it offers a greater advantage still in the opportunity for employment and business enterprise after recovery of health. In many of the famed health resorts there is nothing but the dwelling houses and the sanatorium on some isolated mountain side. When the patient is again able to resume his work in life, he is forced to return from his health-giving resort to the old conditions, exposing himself again to the treacherous climate from which he fled.

Colorado does not cure and then drive out, but rather welcomes the restored invalid, and holds out every inducement for him to remain.

THE VAST RESOURCES OF THE STATE.

These are only beginning to be appreciated. On every side agriculture, fruit raising, mining, all offer a wide field for development and a rich reward for enterprise.

Cripple Creek was for long years only known as excellent grazing country for cattle—till in 1891 it was found to be a gold district of now famous values. To show its wonderful development, the figures of its annual output are given: 1891, $125,000; 1892, $400,000; 1893, $2,500,000; 1894, $4,000,000; 1895, $8,000,000; 1896, 16 tons of gold; 1897, 25 tons of gold. There are other camps, old and new, and many districts yet unexplored, which offer similar opportunities for investment of energy and capital.

The resources of the state in coal and iron are equally great. The coal deposits are of great value, and the area of coal lands surpasses that of Pennsylvania by 8,000 square miles. Pennsylvania has 10,000, and Colorado 18,000 miles.

Agriculture in every branch flourishes and is to-day the foremost industry, offering thus particular inducements to persons of moderate means who ought to follow an outdoor life. In 1895 6,600,000 acres were under cultivation, producing a wheat crop valued at over $4,000,000; alfalfa, $3,500,000; corn, oats and barley, $4,000,000;

with other garden produce at $4,200,000. The production increases yearly.

Under irrigation, with a constant sun, there is no failure of crops, but large and abundant harvests are the rule.

Fruit raising is rapidly becoming an important industry, and the rare quality of Colorado melons and peaches is opening a large market for them in Chicago and St. Louis.

As all of these resources are developed, there comes in consequence more demand in all other lines of business, and new openings are created.

Here, amid civilization and all the advantages of city life and intellectual surroundings, are open country and outdoor life—diversion and fields for occupation. With the restoration of health comes no need for expulsion from this Eden to the old threatening conditions, but a welcome and open opportunities for industry and livelihood.

From start to finish the invalid is at home. There is no exile to foreign lands or strange customs. He is among his own people—in his own land.

"Are not Abana and Phapar better than all the waters of Israel?"

A Few Suggestions.

By B. P. Anderson, M. D., Colorado Springs, Colo.

In calling attention to the Rocky Mountain region and to Colorado in particular as a health resort, there is one point which I should like to bring prominently to the notice of the profession. It can be safely said that one can find in Colorado probably the very best average climate in the world, a climate possessing superior advantages for those afflicted with Pulmonary Diseases; Neurasthenics; cases suffering from lack of tone and vitality due to impoverished blood condition; and from the nature and quality of the atmosphere, (i. e., tonic and antiseptic,) it is most beneficial in all classes of surgical cases. For the conditions noted, any one at all familiar with altitude treatment recognizes its superiority. But the point to which I would call attention and especially emphasize is that the climate is not a "Cure all," and not the much-vaunted panacea with which we are all familiar in patent medicine almanacs and advertisements. And yet speaking from an active professional experience of twenty-five years in Colorado Springs, it is most difficult to say just what classes of cases and stage of disease are most benefited. The reason is obvious. We are not all "built alike." The history and nature of diseases, however similar, cannot always be successfully treated and combatted in any two individuals by routine and the same remedies. This holds good as to climate and its effect upon different individuals who may be suffering with the same disease. Take for instance, two identical cases, identical in every respect as to personal temperament, amount of area of disease involved, symptoms, etc., and the one will improve and recover, whereas the other will lose ground, his symptoms become aggravated. Disease instead of being retarded will advance, and he is ordered to a lower elevation and a different climate, often to his benefit and ultimate recovery.

When a physician, after making his first examination of a patient seeking this climate, advances the positive opinion that he will reap benefit, or on the other hand that he will not be benefited in the least, such a physician does not know what he is talking about, or else he is imbued with the Divine spark or penetration which is an endowment unpossessed by the majority of us.

The safe way would be to advise the patient to remain two or three weeks, watch him closely and at the expiration of this period be entirely governed by the result. When we decide upon the necessity of the patient's remaining, it then becomes important, and most important, to advise and admonish and guide him as to his mode of life. Physicians sending patients to a high altitude do not always impress upon them the fact that the change they are about to make will be a most radical one—that they are going to an elevation of from four to six thousand feet greater than that to which they have been accustomed, and as a consequence an acclimating process will almost of necessity ensue, which will compel them for a time at least, to pursue an entirely different line of living from that to which they were advised at home or at sea level.

Much trouble would be saved and much benefit would accrue to the patient if he were given to understand to start with, that the first effect of a high altitude is one of over stimulation and over work for all of the organs, more especially the heart and lungs, and that as a consequence it will be absolutely necessary that he exercise the greatest care and prudence as to the amount of exercise he may indulge in, and he should make no attempt to get more than a few blocks from his hotel or boarding place for at least the first ten days or two weeks. Much harm and even serious and fatal results attend many invalids seeking this climate, through ignorance upon their part as to the necessity of moderation in exercise. I have known patients coming here, acting upon the advice received at home to "rough it" and "take all the exercise in the open air you can stand," start off immediately endeavoring to take in the whole Pike's Peak region in a single day. One barely takes the time to brush off the dust of travel before he orders a saddle horse or carriage, or starts out on foot for a long jaunt, following advice and congratulating himself that he is at last in a climate which enables him to keep in the open air. The first effect of his change to a high altitude is one of exhilaration, both physical and mental. He hugs the delusion that he is rapidly regaining health and on the high way to permanent recovery. By his indiscretion as to exercise the necessary reaction comes only too quickly and he finds himself prostrated with perhaps a strained heart, high temperature and an active renewal of hostilities and extension of disease from a partial or completely arrested area. In a climate essentially of dry air and sunshine such as that of Colorado, the manner of living by the phthisical patient would seem to require no suggestion—remain as much as possible in the open air and sunshine, most certainly. But live at first as indicated, quietly, and be content to become accustomed to the change before attempting exercise inducing the least fatigue.

The average invalid comes fully armed and imbued with the one idea to get as much air as possible. In truth to "get his money's worth." This patients must do in as short a time as possible. They have come to live out of doors and the number and depth of inspirations are commensurate with their early recovery. They are following instructions. The family physician may or may not give them a pocketful of prescriptions but in any event rarely fails to impress upon them the importance of exercise; "rough it", "live out of doors," "ride horse back," "climb the mountains." In truth, do everything but keep quiet. Again the average patient does not consider that he or she makes the change of climate for health instead of pleasure. Often new comers devote themselves to the social phase of life, which is almost or quite as detrimental as lack of moderation in exercise—of course I mean this is true when they first come and before they become acclimated or until the disease has become arrested.

I am aware that I make a bold assertion, but nevertheless a true one when I state that I have seen during my residence in Colorado, very nearly as many cases of phthisis which we would designate curable, fail of recovery, simply from imprudence in the matter of exercise and indiscretion in the manner of living, as those cases of extensive lesion which rendered recovery absolutely impossible and which are termed incurable.

Dr. Tucker Wise, in his work upon Alpine winter in its medical aspects, writes: "Another question of equal importance is the amount of exercise that should be indulged in by the new comers; the counsel given to keep in the open air as much as possible may, if incautiously followed out on arrival, abridge some of the advantages to be gained during the first month's sojourn." Again, "There is too much eagerness displayed by the novice to rush up the mountain sides or take prolonged exertion." "This if it does not lead to anything more than fatigue or loss of appetite will be a bad economy of time for the rate of improvement will certainly be retarded." Patients from the over stimulation feel better, frequently imagine that they are entirely recovered, can see no reason why they cannot do as much as any one, and as a consequence indulge in excesses which are followed by disastrous and grave results.

I am convinced that the consumptive invalid requires the same amount of supervision and care and restriction as an irresponsible child. This is the more manifest when we consider the hopeful nature of the disease, the almost invariable conviction of improvement and the usual tendency to belittle, if not entirely to ignore, symptoms. He is inclined to over-estimate strength, almost invariably failing to recognize the necessity of rest and quiet.

To the new-comers I would urge for the first few weeks moderation in exercise no matter what the variety or specific nature of the disease or the amount of area of tissue involved. In those cases of elevated temperature, increased pulse rate, rapid or difficult respiration, the importance of absolute rest and quiet is of the utmost necessity. As urgent symptoms disappear, exercise may be indulged in, short walks or drives,—always keeping in view the great importance of never carrying the exercise to the point of fatigue.

In Colorado Springs there can always be found in the parks and other portions of the town, benches and comfortable seats affording suitable resting places of which invalids may always avail themselves.

To conclude, I should advise the invalid as his symptoms lessen and disappear, and his disease becomes arrested, gradually to extend his exercise, each day increasing his walk or drive, keeping in the open air during the hours from 10 a. m. to 4 p. m. during the majority of the winter days—and for many days during the summer months living in a tent, would be a most advantageous regimen.

Colorado climate is not a cure-all; neither is it perfect, but it will average twenty-five days of sunshine in each month, allowing the invalid to be out of doors, and if one regains health and recovers, it produces a permanent recovery, permitting residence (with restrictions of prudence and care as to avoidance of atmospheric changes,) in any portion of the country, as evidenced by the number of recovered patients who have returned to their homes in various portions of the East and who to-day, after many years have elapsed, are in perfect health.

Some Facts Concerning ..... Colorado Springs.

(From Transactions of the Colorado State Medical Society, 1897.)

By R. K. Hutchings, M. D., Colorado Springs.

It is not the object of this paper to vaunt new remedies or compile statistics of wonderful cures. It is in more homely guise. It is written more for the benefit of those who are non-residents and have perhaps heard but little of our place. Many a person in the Eastern and Central States imagines that in the wild and bibulous West we have no civilized and refined attractions, and that an insurance policy will come in handy to him who is foolhardy enough to venture among us. This paper will endeavor to show why such an opinion is wrong, and induce a desire to visit us and share our comforts and joys.

Colorado Springs is a thriving town of over 22,000 inhabitants, with more coming every day. One may walk upon the streets for many days and never see an Indian or a fiercer man than a policeman. Nearly every nationality is represented. The peaceable Chinaman pursues the even tenor of his way by the side of the harmless Anglomaniac with his golf club. Tall, angular Americans, sturdy Englishmen, brawny Scotchmen, swarthy Spaniards, Mexicans, Germans, Jews, Greeks, etc., in fact, the representative of any race you may name, can be seen jostling one another in the busy traffic of the street every day. A person speaking any language can come here and find an interpreter without difficulty. Our social life is as many-hued. It varies from the man who has no social position to maintain, to him who is the embodiment of all that pedigree and wealth can produce. The snob and the gentleman, the swell and the hobo, all breathe our life-giving air and thrive upon it.

We have no saloons or gambling houses in the city limits. Three miles distant by electric car in Colorado City or "Old Town" there is a plentiful supply.

We have an able-bodied, active police force. Crime of every description is at a minimum, and contrary to "tenderfoot" ideas, the citizen is not compelled to carry a gun and be a dead shot in order to protect life and property.

Any one religiously inclined has the choice of twenty-six places of worship, all of different denominations and under different leaders. If not of a sectarian turn of mind, it is easy to reach the mountains and canons where nature can be worshipped in all her sublime majesty.

Many people imagine that because Colorado Springs has been a health resort for so many years it is surely a disease-breeding place due to the many invalids resident here. This is a gross error, as is plainly proved by the report made to the Climatological Association in Washington, D. C., last month. It shows conclusively that a person in good health runs a minimum amount of risk of contracting tuberculosis here, as only twenty cases of this disease were contracted here in the last twenty years.

The sanitation is as nearly perfect as can be in a town of this size. There is an ordinance in effect which prohibits all promiscuous expectoration in any public place—in street cars, and on the side walks. All paved walks must be washed every day. The irrigating ditches which line the sidewalks are flushed several times a week, carrying away any refuse matter in them.

Our Board of Health consists of eight members, including four licensed physicians, a sewer and plumbing inspector, and a food inspector. The sewerage system is complete within the city limits, and the inspector rigidly enforces the ordinance in respect to water closets and drainage. The food inspector protects the inhabitants in regard to adulterated foods and impure milk. Every dairy is registered and watched. We have a large dairy which furnishes genuine pasteurized milk to those who are particular as to the amount of micro-organisms they consume.

Contrary to the general public opinion of health resorts, Colorado Springs is not an unpleasant place to live in on account of the invalids present. It is doubtful, were attention not called to it, if a stranger would judge it to be a health resort from the appearance of the majority of the inhabitants. One of the most noticeable features, to a newcomer, is the high color seen in the faces of most of the residents. Our altitude being about 6,000 feet above sea level, the blood comes to the surface of the body and the dilated capillaries cause a rich, red glow, which on a crisp day looks as if "rouge" had been used with unsparing hand. The majority of residents here are not invalids in search of health, but healthy people in search of wealth, as this is one of the headquarters for the Cripple Creek region twenty miles away.

It is a well established fact that high altitudes, up to a certain limit, benefit pulmonary trouble of nearly every description. In the past the great trouble has been to find mountain resorts which could furnish any degree of comfort for the invalid. Some years ago, patients coming to this place were compelled to put up with the poorest accommodations. Today it is different. We furnish all the luxuries of the East, in addition to a climate that is unsurpassed for an all-the-year-around dwelling place. In the winter the air is dry, cool and bracing. No fogs, no dew; no drenching rains, continuing for days at a time, no long continued cold. It is true the thermometer registers, at times, zero and even below, but owing to the dryness of the air and the amount of electricity in it, invalids can go out every day and feel invigorated. This cold does not last more than a few days at a time and the sunshine, which is almost perpetual, quickly asserts its sway and kills the frost king. The heat of the sun's rays in winter is well shown by the streets. On the shady side the snow or frost may remain several days, while on the sunny side the way is dry and warm. There is a distinct line of demarcation between the two about the center of the street, due to the shadow cast by the buildings. In the summer, the sun's rays are very hot. To be comfortable, it is only necessary to ward off the direct rays of the sun by some form of shade, and a cool breeze is then experienced. A hot, sultry day is never found if one keeps in the shade. We have no sunstrokes or heat prostrations. The nights are always cool and a light blanket is necessary, for comfortable sleeping, throughout the entire summer. It is due to our glorious, perennial sunshine, that this place remains healthy, in spite of the number of invalids here. It is amply proved that the tubercle baccilli and spores do not live long in this place. This, coupled with the fact that our health ordinances compel all buildings to be renovated after each invalid has left, keeps the town a pure, healthy spot, for sick and well alike. The exhilarating and health-giving properties of climate are not found alone in Colorado Springs. Nearly the entire state is one grand health resort, as was aptly expressed by a lecturer not long since:—"If a man were to tumble out of the heavens any place over Colorado, he would be sure to drop into a natural health resort, and there would be no doubt but that he would derive some benefits while falling through the air."

· We have so little rain that very few houses have gutters or spouts. Any water that falls is immediately sucked in by the sandy soil. Walking is better after a rain than before it. With all this dryness, we have no lack of water for practical purposes. Miles away, up on our mountains, are vast lakes and reservoirs, kept free from all contamination. This water, summer and winter, is cold and clear as crystal. We use no filters and it is not alkaline. Repeated examinations made by experts show it to be as pure as it looks, free from pathogenic germs. The streets are lined with irrigating ditches, which supply the trees and lawns with ample moisture. These streets are fine stretches of smooth roadway, lined with beautiful shade trees and as level as a floor. Here we have the bicycler's paradise. Our winters do not compel the housing of a wheel. It can be used the whole year through. In 1896 seven days would cover the time during the whole year that a wheel could not be ridden, and these seven days were not consecutive ones. The average precipitation for the past sixteen years, per year, was 14.46 inches.

Our hotel and boarding house accommodations are of the best. They range from a 25-cent lodging house to the finest hostelries. Private rooms can be obtained among the best class of people, and on the most fashionable streets, if so desired. We have restaurants serving 15 to 25-cent meals, and hotels ranking with the best in the land.

Electric street cars carry you from one end of the town to the other, and out to the foot of the mountains and the mouths of the canons. To those who wish it, horses and carriages and traps of all descriptions are to be had at reasonable rates. You can get in or out of town by six different railroads. An efficient telephone service connects the place with Denver, Cripple Creek, Pueblo, Leadville, Canon City, Aspen, and all the intermediate outlying towns.

The streets and most of the houses are lighted by electricity. We possess over a dozen newspapers, daily, weekly and religious, and two large public libraries with reading rooms. The educational advantages are superb—one large college of high grade curriculum; two academies for boys; one academy for girls and young ladies; a school for the deaf and blind; two business colleges; a summer school; a high school; eight district graded schools and two or more kindergartens.

For the care of the sick, are two sanatoria, a hospital, and the Childs-Drexel Home for Union Printers, a large number of scientifically-trained nurses, and over fifty doctors.

In the way of amusement we possess two theaters; several social clubs; a race track for horses and bicycles; several lakes for boating, skating and fishing; a boundless prairie on the east side, where the coyote, jack rabbit and antelope are hunted with horse and hounds; on the west, the Rocky Mountains, where abounds innumerable wild game,—deer, elk, moose, wild cats, bear, mountain sheep, mountain lions, mountain grouse and other varieties. The mountain streams contain the famous gamey trout. During the summer season the lovely Broadmoor Casino is open day and night. Numberless tennis courts occupy vacant lots, and the game can be played almost the entire year; in fact, any out-door game or sport is to be had for the asking, as every one lives out doors and so chooses athletic games.

Five miles to the west is the world-renowned Spa, Manitou. It is here we find the wonderful mineral springs—soda, sulphur, iron, and a combination of all. These mineral waters are used for the treatment of liver, kidney and blood troubles. They are bottled and shipped to all parts of the country for table waters. The soda water in its natural state is impregnated with ginger, and called "ginger champagne." It rivals the famous Belfast ginger ale. The large hotels are filled during the season with the wealth and fashion of the land, all on pleasure bent.

Manitou is reached by a picturesque ride by rail, electric car, horse or bicycle. The route passes the Garden of the Gods, a place of grotesque beauty and known to all. At Manitou, the entrance to Ute Pass appears. This is a magnificent roadway, hewn out of the solid rock, winding up the mountain side, past Rainbow Falls, on a grade of 211 feet to the mile.

In all this surrounding neighborhood many people live all the year round in tents, and live comfortably, too. With an almost cloudless blue sky overhead the entire year, a dry, bracing air surrounding ,and a perfectly dry sandy soil underneath, what is to prevent tenting perennially?

Some years ago the idea was prevalent that children could not live in this altitude. The children themselves have proved the fallacy of this. Children born here of consumptive parents grow up lusty and hale. They live out of doors, summer and winter; and the bacillus has no chance for its life. The tubercle bacillus dries up and blows away dead. The children here are so numerous that it was necessary to build new schools and enlarge the old ones. A healthier lot of young ones can be found in no clime or country. No, dear readers, when you come to Colorado Springs, you are not coming to a consumptive-ridden town in the backwoods, where you will drag out a weary existence and your children die from inanition. You come to a land that is practically flowing with milk and honey. The milk is pure and the honey contains no glucose, as it is cheaper than the glucose itself, it is unprofitable to adulterate it.

The great fault to be found with invalids on their arrival at Colorado Springs is the haste displayed in taking in the sights. It is a positive fact that the majority of tubercular cases with hemorrhagic tendencies do well in this altitude. But it is equally true that these cases should not go to the top of Pike's Peak the first week of their sojourn here. Any physician sending tubercular cases here should warn them of the dangers attendant upon much exertion during the first two weeks at least. These dangers are hemorrhage and congestion of the lungs. This air is so exhilarating, the sunshine so inviting, and the places of interest so numerous and beautiful, that even a healthy person is very apt to overtax the strength. It takes from a week to a month for the circulatory system to regulate itself. The rare air requires deeper breathing than in a low altitude. Until the system accommodates itself to this change in density of air, too much muscular exertion is very detrimental. The invalid, the first week here, should not stir from the immediate vicinity of home. The vast majority would do much better, gain health and strength faster, if they spent the first week quietly in bed. This would give the nerves, heart, and entire body a chance to become accustomed to the change. Then by gradually increasing the open air exercise, there would be no shock, and the chances of hemorrhage are even less than in a low altitude. Numberless hemorrhagic cases come here and are cured.

In regard to cases of consumption, it may be well to state here that the vast majority of cases come here in the second and third stages. In a few instances, patients have come here on stretchers, have rallied, and lived for years. No Colorado doctor advises the bringing of such desperate cases, as the odds of life are against them and the fatigues of the journey generally hasten the end. The time to send them here is in the incipiency of the disease; then a cure can be looked for.

Two of our disagreeable possessions are wind and dust. We have both at times, but the duration is short and visitations far between. Our winds are rarely over forty miles per hour, and the force is much less than in lower altitudes, in proportion to the pressure of the atmosphere which is about one-fifth less here than at sea level. The dust is a minor factor here, as we have street sprinklers, electric and otherwise. None of the storms last over a few hours, and afterwards the air is purer than before.

Little mention has been made of the numerous canons and wild mountain scenery in this immediate vicinity. Each holiday and on Sunday the town is depopulated, the Mecca being Manitou, the canons, Garden of the Gods, and numerous other scenic resorts. The fact that the old residents, as well as visitors, are in this exodus shows the never-failing interest of these places. Street cars, horses, carriages and bicycles are all pressed into service, and the whole town goes on a grand picnic at every opportunity.

Every hour of the day shows a change in the beauty of the mountains. The tints and general appearance are kaleidoscopic. These hues are the despair of painters. The greens, grays, and purples are so blended that it is impossible to re-produce them. Some days Pike's Peak looks as if within a hand's breadth of the town; the weather bureau building at the summit and the cog-road up the side can be distinguished. Again it is miles away, and appears as if reaching to the very gates of Heaven, now covered with clouds, again, a pure white, glistening in the sun or moonlight.

The canons mentioned above are rocky gorges cleft in the mountains, a stream and roadway at the bottom, and on either side precipitous granite walls hundreds of feet in height. The three principal ones are North Cheyenne, South Cheyenne and Williams Canons. Far up in South Cheyenne foam Seven Falls, made famous in history and song. At the summit, on the mountain side, was the grave of Helen Hunt Jackson, a spot sought out by tourists from far and near. In the upper end of North Cheyenne is seen Silver Cascade Falls—a waterfall flowing over a smooth granite base appears as a sheet of silver suspended in the clear air. And Williams Canon contains the wonderful Cave of the Winds. These canons do not depend upon the special spots named for their interesting points; they present a panamora of interest from beginning to end, and are natural picnicking and camping grounds. A hundred visits would not exhaust their beauties or reveal all their charms.

All physicians know that to successfully administer to a body diseased it is necessary to buoy up and interest the mind. Colorado Springs furnishes this buoy in hundreds of other attractions than those above named. We have an ideal health resort, and desire all physicians to investigate thoroughly what we offer. Differing from a majority of health resorts, we keep "open house" all the year around. Our season lasts twelve months, so it is possible for an invalid to come here with his or her family and live the balance of a lifetime. Many fine houses and medium houses can be rented here already furnished. Extortionate prices are not in vogue as in summer resorts, where it is necessary to make enough money in three months to live on the other nine. To quote the familiar words of the advertisements, "before going elsewhere, or sending patients elsewhere, we invite you to call or write and see what we have, as we are not afraid of close investigation."

The Early Recognition and the Climatic Treatment of Pulmonary Tuberculosis.

(From "The Medical News.")

By H. B. Moore, M. D., Colorado Springs, Colo.

Each year's added experience with the high altitude treatment of pulmonary tuberculosis impresses me freshly with the idea that certain very elementary facts relating to this very valuable therapeutic method, although often detailed by interested students of the subject, are constantly lost sight of by physicians prescribing this mode of treatment. The most important of these relates to an early recognition of the true nature of the case, so that the altitude treatment may be instituted at once, and to the desirability of a more or less prolonged residence at the high altitude. Disregard of reasonable forethought in these particulars, more especially the first point, leads to great disappointment on the part of patients and friends and brings undeserved disrepute upon the treatment. I am willing to admit that some of the blame for this should rest upon the shoulders of too enthusiastic admirers. A goodly portion of it, however, belongs properly to that large body of practitioners who no sooner read of a new cure than they proceed to try it indiscriminately upon every case of the malady coming under their observation.

What is true of other diseases and their medical treatment is also true of the climatic therapeutics of pulmonary tuberculosis. It is far from wise to send every such case to Colorado to try the high altitude treatment. The prospect for an arrest or cure of this disease diminishes very rapidly with its advance, and what has been a most favorable case may soon become inappropriate for this climate. Prophylaxis is always better than cure, and the family physician, seeing a rapidly growing boy or girl with imperfect chest-development, in a family predisposed to tuberculosis, can often avert a catastrophe by sending the child to a high altitude. The out-door life, sunshine and rarefied air of these regions are the most rational and perfect preventives of which one can conceive. Such cases are common in the experience of all physicians, and a practical recognition of the truth of this statement will lead to most gratifying results.

When too late for prophylaxis, and the disease is actually in progress, it seems to me (and my experience in this line has been such as to create strong convictions on the subject) almost criminal to keep the patient at home trying cough-medicines, creosote, guaiacol, cod-liver oil, hypophosphites, etc., during that valuable time, often so short, when climatic treatment is really capable of rendering radical assistance in the struggle with the invading enemy; but, alas, often, one might say usually, the patient is kept at home until the vital powers are weakened by advanced disease, and then, finally, it is decided to send the patient somewhere for his health. Is this reasonable, and can anyone who has the slightest grasp of the subject imagine, for an instant, that any climate will materially help a considerable percentage of cases of this kind? The system is already poisoned with the products of suppuration, and each day finds the cells less able to cope successfully with the already existing disease-area, to say nothing of its spread. This phlegmatic conception and management of tuberculosis is not rational and can never succeed.

One must have a sharp, clear-cut appreciation of the fact that a great danger menaces every individual whose tissues have become the site of the slightest degree of this form of bacterial invasion, and that, although some subjects are found to possess a remarkable degree of tolerance for the disease, as a rule the existence of any considerable amount of tuberculosis tissue in the lungs constitutes a handicap too great for Nature to oppose successfully.

One error probably oftener fallen into than any other, even by physicians, is the idea that a person who looks well, or fairly so, cannot have tuberculosis. They cannot harmonize the appearance of an apparently healthy person before them with their conception of the pale and wan tuberculous patient, and forget that tuberculosis is a disease, which, like other diseases, has a beginning as well as an end, and if the symptoms are suspicious they think their science is at fault and call the disease "bronchitis" or a "cold that lingers," instead of by its right name. It would be interesting to know when, in the opinion of a large number of our professional brethren, these ailments ceased and actual tuberculosis began. I have had the misfortune to see large numbers of self-deceived, or doctor-deceived, human beings with tuberculosis cavities, hectic fever, etc., arrive in Colorado Springs as cases of "bronchitis," "protracted cold," etc., and die in due time. On the other hand, it is a real satisfaction to examine some of the patients sent to Colorado by men thoroughly conversant with the subject, who make an early diagnosis and act on it at once. As a case in point, of which I am glad to say there are many, that of a young man, already becoming well known in our own profession, comes to mind. He had been an athlete in college, and on arrival in Colorado Springs was a picture of healthy vigor, broad, full-chested, and with a good, healthy color; yet a little suspicious cough existed and examination of the chest revealed beginning slight trouble at an apex, and the sputum-examination showed quite numerous tubercle-bacilli.

Cases in which the tuberculous infection is discovered early, and there is scarcely more than a little infiltration at the seat of invasion, are ideal, and may be taken as models of what we should strive after. Often Nature comes to our aid and declares, by means of a small hemorrhage or a slight spitting of blood, that tuberculous invasion has occurred at some little point in a person who has not previously coughed or been unwell in any way. Such an occurrence, although very alarming to the patient, is really a most fortunate one if properly interpreted and acted upon by the physician. Very often, however, the doctor discovers at some point in the throat (usually) or the bronchial tubes the seat of alleged congestion, which he assures the patient caused the bleeding, and encourages the latter not to be alarmed, and so the probably valuable significance of the warning is lost and not thought of again until its repetition, or warnings of another character throw unpleasant light on the subject.

It may be asked with propriety whether the very early cases are the only ones that it is wise to send to a high altitude, and whether conditions so efficacious in prophylaxis and in the early stage of the developed disease are without efficacy in cases that are further advanced on first seeking advice as to the advisability of a change of climate. The reply to this question would be that the high altitude treatment is the treatment suited especially to the earlier manifestations of the disease, the subjects of which still retain a large amount of their accustomed vigor and are able to avail themselves fully of the advantages of out-door life in mountainous climates, which, from the very nature of things, are not very equable and which require a considerable amount of hardness to withstand temperature-changes readily perceived by delicate anemics and subjects of hectic fever. At the same time every physician with experience in elevated regions can recall many cases presenting relatively extensive areas of disease in subjects possessing a considerable degree of tolerance for the disease and free from fever, who thrive in these regions and live many years.

Actual cure, however, is rare in these cases, the disease being merely arrested and liable to begin afresh on return to damp, sea-level climates. A very extensive area of even inactive disease would constitute a decided contra-indication to the high altitude treatment, as a considerable amount of good, healthy breathing space is necessary for a patient to obtain the requisite amount of oxygen in a rarefied atmosphere. It is rarely wise to send active febrile cases advanced beyond the first stage to a high altitude. The deeper breathing required and the exciting character of the climate are very likely to promote destruction of existing consolidation and increase fever. Many such cases are seen in Colorado, in which, so far from being aided, the end is undoubtedly hastened.

As regards the other point to which I wish to call particular attention, viz., the necessity of a more or less prolonged residence at high altitudes, it is a serious error to give a patient going to

Colorado on account of tuberculosis the idea that he is simply to go there for "two or three months," or "to spend the winter." It is very rarely that expectations of this sort can lead to anything but disappointment, and as the disease is of such an essentially chronic character that this length of time is scarcely more than sufficient to furnish an idea as to the probable efficacy of the climate in an individual case.

Right here arises a question that it is often difficult to answer, viz., when is a patient cured of pulmonary tuberculosis and when is the disease only arrested and completely inactive? and yet it is, to the last degree, important for the patient to have this question answered correctly if he wants to return home. Some might say that a case may be looked upon as cured when the cough and expectoration have ceased entirely, when rales have disappeared from the chest, and the weight and general bodily functions have become normal; but it is a matter of every-day experience that under such conditions the patient frequently again begins to expectorate bacilli-laden sputa and to exhibit all the symptoms of renewed activity, showing that the disease was not cured and that the tissues had constantly contained live bacilli and larger or smaller areas of tubercle ready to soften at the proper time. It seems, therefore, as a rule, much wiser for the physician at home to be very conservative upon this point and to instil into the patient's mind, from the first, the idea that the contemplated change of climate, if found on trial to meet the patient's needs, must be a long and perhaps permanent one. If the patient hears this for the first time from his new physician after leaving home, he is naturally surprised at the lack of accord between this advice and what he had been led to believe previously, and feels home-sick and unprepared for so radical a change in his plans.

The desirability of the change of climate being very long or permanent is especially manifest when the patient is right in the midst of what might be called the most vulnerable age; when physique and family tendencies all indicate a subject of pronounced susceptibilities. Under these circumstances a premature return home after arrest or cure (?) might lead to a fatal relapse. Colorado Springs has to-day hundreds of citizens who have lived here for years with a good practical degree of health, enjoying their share of the activities and pleasures of life, and yet they are not cured of their tuberculosis and could not return to their former homes with safety. Many others have been completely cured and could live anywhere, but remain here from choice and the growth of local interests.

With respect to this point of prolonged residence our American high altitudes in Colorado possess most conspicuous advantages over high altitude resorts abroad, like Davos Platz, St. Moritz, etc., which are purely and simply health resorts, offering no opportunities for occupation to those who need it and having no permanent society or home-life. In short, a young tuberculous person who has been sent sufficiently early in the disease to Colorado soon finds that he has not been consigned to a health resort for life, but that he has simply changed his residence to another portion of the country filled with communities with many attractions, where work and a career still await him. It must not be inferred from these statements that Colorado has more positions than people to fill them or that it is especially easy to get remunerative employment, for such is not the case. On the contrary, the unemployed poor are found here as everywhere; but it is meant that talent and ability in all lines can find scope for their exercise here as promising as elsewhere, now, and with an encouraging prospect for future growth, often absent in the Eastern States. The lot of the very poor, who are at the same time ill, is a hard one anywhere, and must remain so until means are devised by the State or by individuals to relieve this most distressing form of need.

Extracts
from Writings of S. E. Solly, M. D.,

OF COLORADO SPRINGS.

I. FROM "MEDICAL CLIMATOLOGY."

(Publishers: Lea Bros., Philadelphia.)

Climates of High Altitudes.—These are all well represented by reports of the cases of 2.027 patients who resided in the Alps and 571 who were treated in Colorado, making a total of 2,598. The Alps had five reporters and Colorado four. No reports could be obtained from other high climates. The Alpine percentage for all stages is 3 per cent. higher, which slight difference is apparently due not to any superiority of climate, but to a higher percentage of first-stage cases in the Alpine than in the Colorado reports (Alps 60 per cent. in the first stage, and Colorado only 40 per cent.)

It is probable that the cases were also better selected and the patients more prudent.

If we extract the percentages of results for all stages of each group and put them in order, progressing from the ocean up to the high altitudes, we see an almost steady rise in the percentage of improvement as we proceed toward the highlands, as illustrated by the chart.

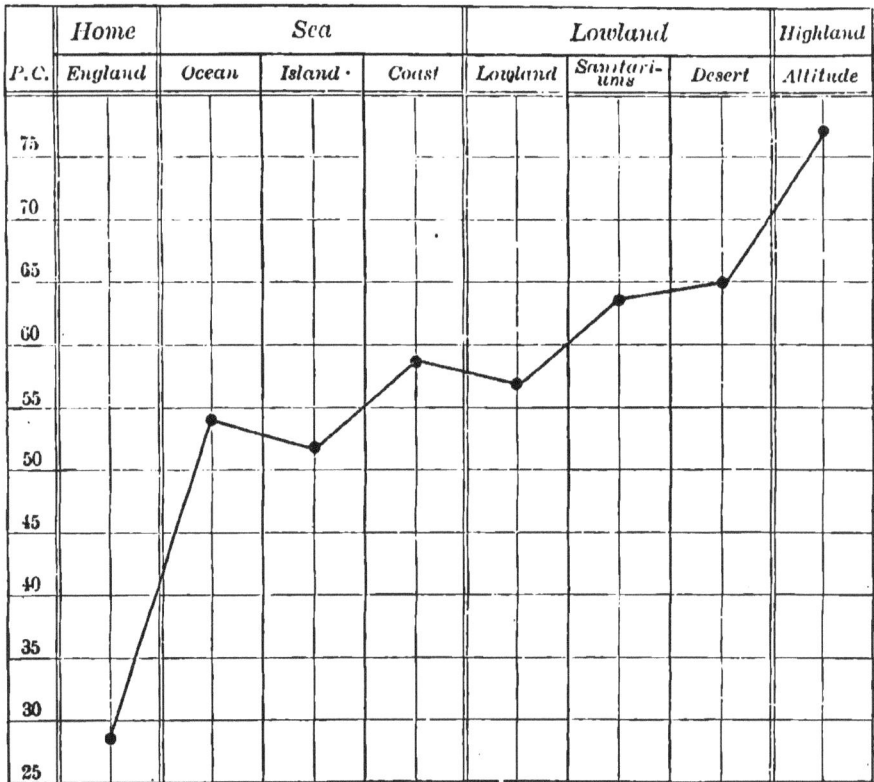

P.C.	Home	Sea			Lowland			Highland
	England	Ocean	Island ·	Coast	Lowland	Sanitari-ums	Desert	Altitude
75								
70								
65								
60								
55								
50								
45								
40								
35								
30								
25								

Influence of Sea-air.—In making a further analysis of the reports it will be seen that two chief climatic factors exert apparently the greatest influence upon the results, namely, sea-air and mountain-air. If we arrange the reports into three groups, the first consisting of the ocean, the island, and the coast climates (England being omitted, as it does not illustrate climatic change); the second group, composed of the low inland climates, with the sanitariums and the desert climates; and the third, formed of all the high altitude reports, and then compare their total percentages of benefit, we find they range in the following order:

	All stages.	1st stage.	2d and 3d stages.
Sea climates,	57 per ct.	71 per ct.	38 per ct.
Inland climates,	63 "	92 "	57 "
Climates of high altitude,	76 "	89 "	63 "

This shows improvement as the sea-influence diminishes. There is an exception in the first stage cases in the second group, which is doubtless due to the special selection of the cases before admission to the sanitarium and to the extra care taken of them while there.

Influence of Altitude.—In order to show the influence of high altitudes as compared with that of low altitudes, I have combined all the low altitudes, viz.: Ocean, island, coast, inland sanitariums, and desert together and contrasted the total percentage with that obtained in high climates. The result is as follows:

	All Stages.	1st Stage.	2d and 3d Stages.
Low climates	59 per cent.	75 per cent.	47 per cent.
High climates	76 per cent.	89 per cent.	63 per cent.

This inquiry has clearly demonstrated two things, viz.: That the majority of consumptives do better, other things being equal, the further they are removed from the sea, and that they do better in high than in low altitudes, wherever situated, the difference in proportionate improvement being here exhibited.

The rainy months are from April to August inclusive, the most protracted season being usually a period of four or six weeks of daily rains, beginning during the last half of July. In the mountains these rains are more severe, but on the plains they frequently amount only to afternoon thundershowers.

The total yearly rainfall averages 14.46 inches; of this the normal precipitation is 11.18 inches during the five months from April to August, inclusive, leaving 3.28 inches to fall during the remaining seven months from September to March, inclusive. "It therefore follows that the fall of snow is infrequent and scanty through the winter. By reason of the dryness and porosity of the soil and the dryness of the air, with the warmth and almost constant sunshine, the evaporation of snow is very rapid. In looking at the temperature-record it will be noticed that once or more during the winter the temperature drops below zero, and sometimes a long way below. Such temperatures rarely last throughout the day, as the sun seldom fails to shine. When such cold weather occurs during the day the wind, instead of taking its usual daily course from north to south through the eastern quarter, remains in the north, but has a small velocity, a high wind and low temperature being rarely met in conjunction. On these exceptional days the younger and more vigorous invalids go out to exercise with benefit, but those who are more delicate remain indoors, bearing their captivity with grace, as something that occurs to them only three or four days out of the whole winter. Driving is most agreeable in the morning, as there is usually very little wind; but after luncheon a strong breeze from the southeast is not uncommon, making walking or riding more pleasant."

June is likely to be one of the most suitable of the summer months for camping-out, as there are usually several weeks of dry, sunny weather before the coming of the cooling summer-rains.

The mornings are invariably fine during the entire year, and are therefore the most favorable time of the day for being outdoors.

A few hot days occur during the summer, but the nights in these high altitudes grow rapidly cooler toward morning. "The absence of dew permits all but the most delicate invalids to sit on porches in the evening with enjoyment."

The autumn and winter are delightful, the sun usually shining strong and clear and warm, even after a night when the mercury has dropped pretty low. The air is so dry in winter that during the "invalid's day" lasting from 9 to 4 o'clock the temperature outdoors in the sun is rarely uncomfortable.

The ground is usually bare of snow, no rain falls from mid-September to mid-April, and the sun shines unobstructed by clouds. During the three winter months the number of cloudy days does not average more than five a month. The effect of such an air is bracing and genial, and being so dry the cold in the shade is very little felt, a medium-weight wrap being all that is needed. The roads are good and seldom obstructed by snow or mud, and the neighboring hills and plains are full of interesting points to visit, and pleasant, sheltered nooks where the invalid can rest under the agreeable heat of the sun and eat his midday meal without fear of taking cold."

Colorado Springs possesses advantages such as few other resorts can offer; a dry, porous gravel-soil; unusually wide streets; town-sewerage; remarkably pure, soft mountain-water, containing less than three grains of total solids to the gallon; and good drives, beautiful natural scenery, and the absence of manufactories.

The markets are surprisingly good in Colorado Springs. The

grocery, provision, and fruit-stores are numerous and unusually well supplied for a town of this size.

The summers in Colorado Springs are usually cool. In 1892 there were eleven days when the thermometer rose above 90 degrees, the highest point being 94 degrees; in 1893 there were two days above 90 degrees, the highest temperature being 93 degrees; in 1894 a temperature of 90 degrees was reached on one day only; in 1895 there were no days over 90 degrees, the highest temperature being 89 degrees.

In the warm days that occur in Colorado Springs the air is invariably dry. When the temperature goes above 85 degrees the relative humidity usually drops below 25 per cent., and the "sensible" temperature is about 60 degrees. The mean of the summer minima is 51 degrees, showing cool nights.

There are severe wind-or dust-storms at infrequent intervals when the air is very dry and electrical. They are exceedingly disagreeable, but do not occur more than half a dozen times a year, and the greatest violence of the wind rarely lasts more than a few hours. The gravel-soil of the plain on which the town of Colorado Springs stands greatly mitigates this annoyance as compared with that experienced in towns built on adobe-soil.

II. FROM "INVALIDS SUITED FOR TREATMENT IN COLORADO SPRINGS."

The most marked benefit is shown in antagonizing and arresting tuberculosis in those whose ancestry or physique, or both, convey the impression of their being affected with general tuberculosis.

Hemorrhagic cases are found to do well.

Phthisis consequent upon croupous pneumonia, or pleurisy, is generally benefited.

The presence of a cavity is not, in itself alone, a bar to coming and receiving good.

Fibroid phthisis is usually improved.

Cases of so-called catarrhal pneumonia generally do well, but where there is a marked tendency to acute febrile catarrhs of the tubes, or a specially irritable and useless cough, a more medium climate is indicated.

Rapid progress and pyrexia are not contraindications, if there is evidence of a sufficiency of healthy lung remaining and if the patient is able to take and assimiliate enough food, and shows a fair power of reacting to stimulation by cold, and a capacity toward recuperation from fatigue.

Very moderate dilatation of the heart in the young is not a positive preventative, if care is exercised. Nor is old valvular disease, if tolerated with and compensated for.

Albuminuria caused by lardaceous disease would be a decided contraindication. Any renal complication makes the experiment of change to Colorado extremely risky for precipitating the end, though chronic Bright's disease, without pulmonary disease also, is usually favorably influenced.

Chronic catarrh and inflammation of the throat, nose, or bronchi, are generally improved, and even tubercular laryngitis is, per se, not contraindicated.

To sum up as regards the individual, the anaemic and phlegmatic are best influenced as regards the disease; the chronic, as regards the stage of disease.

A larger margin of sound tissue in the peccant organ is demanded than in changing to a less extreme climate, and a certain evidence of vital resiliency is imperative.

With respect to pulmonary disease, let it be especially remembered that in sending your patients to Colorado, you are putting them, as it were, in a gymnasium, and they will need prudence and instruction to benefit by it; that the whole principle of the influence of altitude upon chronic disease is the exciting of a healthy life in the place of an unhealthy, and that in the process there comes the strain of the battle; that in prescribing an altitude, to insure success, as in prescribing the most powerful remedies from the Pharmacopoeia, the method of administration demands our most careful consideration.

Taking the medical profession throughout the world, it is unquestionable that a large majority of those who have made a study of the subject believe that where a change is made, a change to an elevated country is the most likely to benefit a consumptive.

The population of Colorado, which grows rapidly, is evidence of its general merits as a resort for consumptives, and this especially applies to Colorado Springs, the healthiest, most agreeable, and accessible town in that country. There are places that are warmer or more sheltered, better suited for some. There are places that are lower or higher, better suited for others. For an average case of phthisis, however, this resort contains a greater number of advantages, both climatic and general, for residence, taking the year round, than any other now accessible.

To build up statistics of cases to prove the merits of Colorado

Springs might not be difficult, but they would be misleading. A number of cases come only to die. A good climate being like a good doctor's practice: there is mortality among his patients, out of proportion to his skill, because he is the resort of the desperate. And, again, there is no country where the invalid fool is more surely and quickly punished for his neglect of good advice, so that, though I hope at some future time to present certain clinical records for your consideration, I will not attempt to build a monument with them to the curative power of this resort. I would rather ask you to look around among our numerous recuperated invalids now living in Colorado Springs or back in their old homes, and reply "Si Monumentum queres circumspice."

III. FROM "THE COMPARATIVE MERITS OF RESORTS IN NEW MEXICO, COLORADO AND ARIZONA."

The statistics show an almost steady rise in the percentage of improvement from the ocean to the altitudes. The percentage of improvement among those who took sea voyages was 54 per cent.; in lowland climates, 57 per cent.; in lowland desert climates, 65 per cent.; while in altitudes the improvement runs up to 77 per cent. From this we learn two things: that as a rule the consumptive improves the further he is removed from the sea influence, as shown in the contrast of the percentage of fifty-four and sixty-five; and further, the benefit of altitude over lowlands, even in desert life, is shown by the difference between sixty-five and seventy-seven. Therefore, while the desert air of Arizona will cure more cases of consumption than the sea air of the coast, say of Southern California, yet it will not cure as large a proportion as will the mountain air of the highlands.

In deciding what cases are exceptions to these general rules, it will be well roughly to classify cases of phthisis as follows: First, those in whom the tendency to the spread of tuberculosis is the most prominent symptom, which may be called, for convenience, the tuberculous cases. Second, those consumptives in whom there is an especial tendency towards inflammatory processes, and those persons are usually of the erethic temperament; this group may be termed the pneumonic. The third division is those in whom there are catarrhal tendencies of a relaxed or low inflammatory type. Such cases are usually anemic and have phlegmatic temperaments. This group may be termed the catarrhal. It is, of course, understood that all are tuberculous, and most have some tendency towards inflammation or catarrh, or both.

As in the tuberculous cases the important matter is to destroy the germs and remove the anemia, it follows that these cases should be placed on high ground where the air is not only dry and sunny but also cool and stimulating. When the patient is able to exercise, the cooler air, such as found during the winter in most resorts of Colorado, is most desirable, and the cure progresses more certainly and rapidly. The cold acts more beneficially than heat upon the usually depressed nervous system of this class of cases, and also induces greater appetite and increased vitality. When the patients are too feeble to exercise, it is sometimes best to begin their cure in a warmer and lower climate, and later to transfer them to the higher and cooler regions.

The extent of lung involved plays an important part in determining the elevation most beneficial to the patient. If marked dyspnea, due to the extent of the lung involvement and not to the anemia or weak cardiac muscle, is present at sea-level, a case with this symptom must be kept on low ground. This particularly applies to obstruction in the left lung.

In comparing Rocky Mountain resorts, it may be said that Colorado Springs possesses the most stimulating, and Yuma the least stimulating, climate.

The winter and fall climate of all these places is good, and is more bracing the greater the altitude, and the higher the latitude.

The spring weather in New Mexico and in Arizona is, as a rule, much better than that in Colorado.

The summers on the high ground of Colorado are cooler and pleasanter, and they are as dry as those of like elevations in New Mexico and in Arizona, where the resorts of moderately low elevation are impossible, on account of excessive heat.

There is generally more wind in the more northerly and elevated resorts; the dust, however, is more objectionable in the more southerly and lower resorts, because the soil is usually adobe (clay) and alkaline, and so rises steadily in the form of a light irritating powder, while on the high ground the soil is more apt to be gravel or granitic detritus.

Is Consumption Contagious.

The Extraordinary Exemption From the Disease in the High Altitudes of Colorado.

(From "The New York Sun.")

By C. F. Gardiner, M. D., Colorado Springs, Colo.

With the present agitation in many of our large cities concerning the extension and spread of that dread life destroyer, consumption, with health boards passing laws against spitting in streets and public places, with cattle being killed by the hundreds to prevent tubercular meat infection and with legislative bodies gravely considering the advisability of laws to quarantine the consumptive invalid, it seems rather a gratuitous question to ask if consumption is contagious. Of course it is contagious. The proof is overwhelming. Men of the highest scientific and technical skill in all civilzed countries have for years proved by direct experiments upon animals and from statistics collected in the study of mankind, that the germ from the dried sputum of consumptives, wafted about in the air, to be inhaled with the dust, or taken in a glass of milk, is capable of giving a person consumption.

The records show it to be a most frequent and deadly disease; one person in every eight dies of it. Take 333 people in any city, and before the year runs out one of them will succumb to this scourge of the human race. The story is the same from the tropical heat of the equator to the cold and frozen north; where people live, there consumption lives also, and claims its victims from the mud hut of the peasant up to the palace of the rich, with an impartial and relentless certainty year after year.

The suffering, the crippled liver, the desolate homes caused by this one disease through the length and breadth of our land, are fearful for one to contemplate; and it is no wonder that scientific men are urging to the utmost any and every drastic measure that will control its spread and stamp it out before its extension becomes a veritable plague to decimate the race.

Is there no escape? Are there no people, is there no race or climate where this awful destroying angel, tuberculosis, is not found? To answer this question one has to turn to climatology, or the study of climate and its effect on mankind. It has long been known that the races inhabiting a country several thousand feet above the level of the sea suffer less from consumption than any others. In the high vales of the Andes it is almost an unknown disease. The same immunity has been found to exist in races living on the high plateaux of the African continent, and the Swiss mountaineers rarely show any evidence of this disease among them. To come nearer home, in our own country throughout the high, dry plateau extending east of the Rocky Mountains, through New Mexico, Arizona, Utah, Colorado, etc., it was observed by the earlier explorers and settlers that consumption was practically unknown. Now that all of this region is becoming rapidly settled, even having cities of fair size, how does this exceptional freedom from this disease hold out? Is this strip of non-tubercular country becoming, like all the rest of the world, infected? Or does the subtle influence of its dry air, sunshine and porous soil give to its fortunate inhabitants, as in the past, an absolute protection from this great man-destroyer, consumption?

If there is such a favored country, let it be known to all. The existence of a natural sanitarium such as this, miles and miles of country bathed in sunshine and pure air, without mankind's worst enemy lurking in every corner—nay, not, as a rule, even present— is a fact that should be shouted from the housetops in every city, town or village over our great country, in which one life in every 333 is lost every year from a contagious and preventable disease.

That consumption will be stamped out by the vigorous action now being taken against it, no one can afford to doubt; but, unfortunately, before that Utopian, non-tubercular era arrives, countless lives will be sacrificed , as contagion is controlled slowly and with great effort, and for years it will be a losing battle. While this is being fought step by step, thousands of childfren are born, children who are weakened by an inherited taint, which is like a spark in a powder magazine. One puff of air comes, and their poorly resisting bodies are all aflame with tubercular fire, a fire smouldering unseen from birth.

A country, then, in which life can be saved, an El Dorado, not of gold, but of health, a country right here in the United States, well called "our natural sanitarium," where to catch consumption is next door to impossible, and where even those who are said to be hopelessly ill with the disease recover, is a country of such a sort that one needs to offer no apology for presenting its merits to the whole world, at once and with all the force one can.

This is not a question of a single section or a boom in corner lots, or even of the seductive and illusive gold and silver mines; it is a question of a nation's health, and deals with a piece of land as big as Europe, in all parts of which the climate offers the same protection and cure— a cure that has stood the test of years, and is, as shown from carefully compiled statistics, more effective in the greatest number of cases than any climate cure ever studied.

There has been, however, for some time, especially in the East, ern cities, considerable alarm expressed about coming to this practically non-tubercular belt for fear that in its towns filled with consumptive invalids there is great danger of contracting the disease. This impression is very strong, is constantly gaining ground, and even doctors are warning their patients not to come to Colorado for that reason. The newspapers have taken it up, and several articles have aopeared; one in the New York Evening Post, which was largely copied, denouncing Colorado Springs as a plague spot and painting the danger and risk of infection from consumption in the most vivid and glowing colors. This article was, no doubt, regarded as true by many people, as it received a wide publicity through the papers all over the country, and, as far as I know, was never denied; so that it probably has been accepted by the average reader as correct.

Now, at first sight, and without positive knowledge to guide one, it cannot be denied that the greatest danger from infection must exist where there are the greatest number of consumptives to com · municate the disease. Other things being equal, it would be so. But other things are not equal, at least in Colorado, and in places with a similar climate, as the factor climate comes in. That makes all the difference, and it was to determine practically this difference between other climates and the climate of Colorado that for some years I have been collecting statistics, and making experiments, so as to take without reserve all the evidence that presented itself on this subjct.

It is estimated beyond doubt that consumption is communicated from the sick to the well by the expectorated matter when it becomes dry and is drawn into the lungs in the form of dust. With a view to ascertaining how communicable the disease is in this climate, I have for a number of years made a careful study of the dust and germs in the air in Colorado Springs and the surrounding country. The air has been analyzed day and night, indoors and out. It was found by these experiments that air all over this elevated region on the prairies, the foothills, and high mountains, was quite free from any germs; in the town itself there was the average number of germs common to any place of like size, increasing in a regular ratio from the thinly-settled portions to the more thickly settled parts, as in other towns; so that the results were negative, with the exception of the wonderful purity of the air everywhere except in the immediate vincinity of human inhabitations.

In the next experiments dust was taken from the walls of rooms occupied by consumptives in houses, hospitals, sanitariums and hotels. The dust was carefully removed from behind pictures, and from similar places, and then injected into animals, which were killed after a certain interval and examined for consumption. These experiments are nearly completed, and will be given to the medical profession at the proper time and place.* The results indicate very clearly that the dust in Colorado Springs at present is not as dangerous as it is under like conditions in a more humid climate, such as that of a town not situated in this dry, elevated region. They also show that a climatic power is at work, which, by first impairing the vitality of the germs, and, secondly, by improving the vitality of the animals, gives a double safeguard against contagion. The animals used in these experiments are freshly imported from Ohio, and since they are not natives represent as nearly as possible the condition of a visitor from the East just arrived in Colorado. It is well to consider this subject of contagion from consumption in Colorado Springs, not only from the point of view of laboratory research, but from a more practical basis, one which any person can understand.

The fact that consumption is transmitted by germs is well established for many cities with other climatic conditions (such as damp soil and greater rainfall), but it is not necessarily true here in anything like the same degree; climate, as I have said, makes all the difference. The physical influence exerted on a man or an animal by the climatic environment due to 200 days of sunshine in the year, fifteen inches annual rainfall, dry sandy soil, and 6,000 feet altitude, when compared with 100 days of sunshine, forty-nine inches annual rainfall, damp clay soil, and no altitude, makes a difference that is a powerful agent for good or bad.

At first sight, however, some factors would seem to favor contagion from consumption in Colorado Springs. There is about one consumptive to every six of the inhabitants. Since the air is dry it hastens the drying of the expectorated matter so that it is more easily carried about in the air. Many of the inhabitants who are

---

*Since published in the Transactions of the American Climatological Association, 1897, and in The American Journal of The Medical Science, February, 1898.

not consumptive are, from family history, probably more prone to contract the disease than the average person. All these facts would seem on their face to point out the danger of contagion; but let us consider the other side of the question.

The germs once on the ground are more rapidly killed by the action of the sunlight, which, coming as it does through a generally cloudless sky and very thin, clear air, acts far more promptly as a disinfectant than in a more humid climate. It is an equally important point that the sun shines here more hours per day than in most places. Even when inhaled into the lungs the tubercular germs are met by a system strengthened and rendered antagonistic to infection by climatic environment. In other words, the climate of all our high, dry plateau renders it more difficult for the germs of consumption to maintain their virulence or to find a suitable soil in the body or lungs for their growth. Now, this is not conjecture on my part. If there is, as has been feared, great danger from contagion in Colorado Springs, surely it is a fact easily observed. The objection cannot be raised, that, like many health resorts, Colorado Springs has only a transient population, and that people who have been infected pass rapidly from observation and do not live long enough here to be reported. Colorado Springs is essentially a city of homes, where people come to live for years; the city has been in existence for twenty years, and the permanent population is large enough to allow one to secure careful statistics.

In 1892 the writer published in the American Journal of the Medical Sciences a report on all the cases of non-imported consumption which had occurred in Colorado for fifteen years. A year was spent in collecting these cases, with their histories. Six of them died. Since that time there have been five more cases. Four of these died, making ten deaths in all, in twenty years. This number is so small as compared to the number in any town of the same size in the United States so as to make it seem unreasonable. The average number of deaths from consumption to each thousand of the inhabitants in most cities is three. But these three deaths, it should be remembered, only represent a small number of the people who contract the disease in that city, as, with the present knowledge of climate cure, a doctor sends his consumptive patients away some little time before death—at least it is to be hoped he does. Many go also of their own accord, and if any of these die, it does not add to the death statistics of their own city, but to those of some health resort. It is, too, a well known fact that death returns are frequently "doctored," and the words tubercular and consumption are not put down for fear of objection on the part of some insurance company, so that three deaths to the thousand per year is clearly no overstatement. It is, in fact, a conservative estimate that these three deaths represent cases of persons who have contracted consumption in the place where they die, as people do not generally go to a city to be cured of consumption.

Therefore, according to statistics, Colorado Springs, with 20,000 inhabitants, should have had last year just sixty deaths from non-imported consumption to put it on a par, as regards danger from contagion, with Boston, New York or Philadelphia. What are the actual facts? Last year but one such death occurred. There was reported to the city physician only one death, and careful inquiry of all physicians and others failed to reveal any more. Nor can it be said that more have occurred and passed unnoticed. The doctors of Colorado Springs are, from necessity, practical specialists in consumption or tuberculosis; they are keenly alive to its detection, and therefore our statistics for that disease bear comparison with those of any city in the country.

This low mortality from consumption contracted in Colorado Springs is not an isolated instance; probably all cities or towns situated on this high, dry plateau would show very much the same record. The city of Denver, seventy-nine miles away, in practically the same climate, illustrates the fact that this place is no exception. Last year Dr. Munn, city physician of Denver, reported sixty-four deaths from non-imported consumption to 150,000 inhabitants, or less than one-half a death to the thousand; and Dr. Sewel, after much research, showed in 1895 a rate in Denver of about one-third of a death per thousand of non-imported consumption.

These facts are not confined to mankind. A general immunity, from living in this country, is also found in domestic animals. In dairy herds, whose general environment, character of food, shelter, and all conditions bearing on general health are far more likely to be the same in any climate than those of man, we have the same result, namely, that consumption in cattle here is most infrequent. Careful reports show that all through a large part of the United States cattle are sacrificed in this plague of tuberculosis or consumption, and the opinion is gaining ground that milk taken from cows so diseased and used as food is in a great measure responsible for many cases of consumption occurring in mankind.

Reports show that from 25 to 50 per cent. of Eastern cattle are tubercular. The report of the state veterinary for Colorado show only 2 per cent. in our herds, when the tuberculin test has been made. The testimony from all over our high plateau, which is from five to eight thousand feet above the sea level, is the same. If, then, it is true that consumption is very often contracted by drinking milk from consumptive cows, this fact that our cows are so remarkably exempt from this disease adds another factor to our safety. If only two cows in the hundred have consumption in Colorado, and twenty-five to fifty in the hundred have it in the East and elsewhere, there is not much room for doubt as to the comparative danger from milk infection. In a drink of milk taken in any of our average cities below 2,000 feet altitude, we run about 30 per cent. more risk of contagion than we do in Colorado Springs.

It may make it plainer if for the sake of comparison I illustrate the truth of some statements I have made by a supposable case. We will, for example, suppose that there is a city or town situated on the Atlantic coast (or anywhere not in this dry, elevated region); a city of 20,000 inhabitants, which has existed for twenty years and increased at a constant ratio of about 1,000 per year; in fact, a town as nearly like this as possible, but without this special climate, and without invalids. Now a man living in this city of the East, with its damp climate, wishes to visit Colorado Springs; he would like to see friends here or the country, or to take a holiday of a month or so, but he fears to come. Why? Because he has heard that there is danger of catching consumption in Colorado Springs; the entire city is crowded with invalids, and he may contract the dread disease by coming in contact with them. So he stays at home, where he feels safe from danger. What are the actual facts? His own city, where he feels so safe from infection, has had during the last twenty years just 630 deaths from consumption (at a ratio of three deaths per 1,000), all, without doubt, contracted, or "caught" in that place. Colorado Springs, where he fears to go, has had ten deaths from consumption, caught here during the same time and with the same population.

These are actual statistics and not based on any guess. Our mortality from consumption contracted in Colorado Springs has been ten deaths in twenty years. A town of the same size and gradual increase of poulation in the East would have had 630 deaths from the disease in twenty years. We stand, therefore, about one-sixty-third as much chance of contracting the disease here as we do in a city of the same size in the East; and any one who fears to leave his home and come out here to live because there is greater danger here, either does not know the actual facts or is very weak on arithmetic, as the ratio of 630 to 10 does not require a mathematical mind to understand, and is so overwhelmingly in our favor as to leave no room for doubt that the danger of contracting the disease here is not based on any fact or truth whatever. I do not stand alone in my opinion regarding the small risk from infection here. I have asked all of the doctors practising in Colorado Springs whose experience extends over a period of some fifteen to twenty years each, and they one and all have expressed themselves as agreeing with me in the conclusion that contagion is a thing of very rare occurrence.

We have seen that practical statistics carefully taken show that consumption does not develope in this high, dry climate to anything like the extent it does elsewhere. Fifty or sixty develope the disease East to one case developed in Colorado Springs, in spite of its consumptive population. Now, why is this? To say that it is due simply to the climate means very little. There are probably many factors. In my opinion this climate, after some twenty days or more, produces a condition of body that resists infection. Lungs that are well used, expanded by deep breaths, so that every cell receives fresh air, are not likely to hold the tubercular baccilli, or allow their growth if they do lodge there. At this altitude the lungs are constantly exercised by deep breathing. Persons whose blood is, as we say, thin or watery, are most liable to consumption. The blood of people living at this altitude is generally thicker than that of people who live at the sea level. The difference is very slight, of course, but thick blood acts more rapidly to destroy germs than thin blood does, and therefore people living here have blood that is inclined to be germ-proof.

As has been shown, the germs of consumption, outside of the body, before they can infect another person have to run the chances of sunlight— a sunlight far stronger and more effective both in point of quality and quantity as a germ-destroyer than most climates have. Furthermore, in eating meat or drinking milk the risk of tubercular infection is, at this altitude, reduced to a minimum, as so few animals are ill with consumption.

Then, quite apart from any scientific reason, there is far more out-of-door life in this climate, and an out-door life is one of the greatest safeguards against taking consumption; so that, although our cases of infection from consumption are so few as to excite wonder and even doubt in many minds, both common sense and science unite to prove very clearly that it is merely a case of cause and effect. The influences acting against infection are many and powerful, and the effect follows of course.

As Colorado Springs grows larger and its inhabitants lead a more sedentary life, as indoor occupations become more frequent and as tall buildings are raised, which shade our streets and shut out sunlight from rooms, we shall be in a much more dangerous position than we are at present, because it is highly probable that as the bad hygienic conditions engendered by over-crowding or by increased population exert their harmful influence, we shall be more and more liable to infection from consumption, and, therefore, it will not do to disregard the precautions which are being taken now to overcome this danger in our large Eastern cities; such measures, even if not so necessary here as elsewhere, do assure people and show them that we are at least keenly alive to the importance of prevention. I can only assert most positively in regard to contagion that there is not at present in Colorado Springs any evidence to show that the risk due to contracting consumption from those ill with the disease is a matter over which the public mind need be disturbed.

Tubercular Infection.

By James A. Hart, M. D., Colorado Springs, Colo.

After about twenty years of experience and fairly careful observation in a general practice in Colorado Springs, I feel that I am warranted in making some statements in regard to what my experience has been in reference to the infectiousness of tuberculosis; also giving some statistics from my own notes in regard to the health of children born here, of tuberculous parents. The observations as I report them are entirely from my own private practice and do not include hospital cases. Without questioning the infectiousness of the disease and with the knowledge that our population is composed almost entirely of families represented by one or more cases of phthisis, I feel that we must possess some aseptic quality in our atmosphere by which to explain the immunity we seem to enjoy from such contagion. During my experience here I have had but one case of pulmonary tuberculosis occur in my own practice that I am positive originated in Colorado. I know of other cases, but my own personal observations are confined to this one case. This case occurred in the person of a lady who had resided in Colorado for several years and was the mother of two healthy children. She came here on account of the health of a sister, who died here of tuberculosis, and had a bad family history. I have had also one case of tuberculosis of the kidney. This was in a married woman. The kidney was removed, she made an excellent recovery, has since given birth to a perfectly healthy child, and is herself the picture of health. She also belonged to a tuberculous family. I am prompted to give my experience on this subject by having seen some articles in both the lay and medical press in which Colorado Springs has been criticised on account of its being infected from its population. I think that my experience coincides with that of most if not all of the members of the profession residing here.

In 1892, after careful inquiry, Dr. Gardiner could only collect and publish ten cases of consumption that had originated here in fifteen years. Since that time he has been able to collect only ten more cases, after having sent a circular letter to all the reputable physicians practicing in Colorado Springs.

Regarding the health of children born in Colorado of tuberculous parents: No one will deny that the children as we see them are remarkably healthy in appearance. In a record of one hundred children born in Colorado Springs of tuberculous parents, I have had three cases of tubercular meningitis in infants under two years of age, and one case at the age of eight years; two cases of hip disease developing at the age of four. I have yet to see a case of pulmonary tuberculosis in a child born in Colorado. My experience with scarlet fever and diphtheria has been limited, but my opinion is that these diseases are less frequently malignant than in Eastern cities. My observations of children born of tuberculous parents in Colorado Springs have included all ages from infancy up to eighteen years.

Rocky Mountain Health Resorts

(From "Western Medical and Surgical Gazette.")

By W. A. Campbell, M. D., Colorado Springs, Colo.

"I was very miserable last summer and fall. The doctor examined my lungs, fearing tuberculosis. Said my left lung needed close watching. I took about a six-months' treatment and am looking and feeling so well, all but a little indigestion. * * * * * * I have talked to our family physician and he thinks it might be a good plan (coming to Colorado),but like some other physicians dislikes the idea of settling in a place where there are so many invalids, especially consumptives. Do you think it would be a great risk?"

The foregoing is from a letter recently received from a lady in West Central Illinois. She came to Colorado during the summer of 1895 with her husband who was suffering from acute tuberculosis. While here I attended her during confinement. Her husband rapidly failed in health. He returned home in October and soon died. From her letter we would infer that she had symptoms of tuberculosis, and there was a question as to whether it would not be the proper thing for her to change climates.

Her doctor does not stand alone in his opinion. Like sentiments are expressed by many physicians in the central and eastern states. We hear it almost daily, through the press and from patients coming to Colorado for their health. We believe our eastern confreres are honest in their opinions, but at the same time we feel they have not given the subject that careful thought or attention it deserves. We are dealing with the earthly destinies of our patients; their worldly interests, their happiness and that of their families, depend upon the advice we may give them. It is well then to give the subject more than a passing glance that we may be able to give the proper advice. We see physicians, earnest in their work, who desire to do the best they can for their patrons, hold their patients at home rather than send them to our health resorts where they suppose there is great danger of contracting tuberculosis. It is our duty to inquire into this matter and see if there be any foundation for the opinions that are abroad in the land.

I trust those who may read will not feel that this paper has been written for gain to the author. A much more elevated feeling has prompted me to inquire into the subject; a desire to enlighten the physicians of the eastern states with facts bearing on the subject, and to point out to them the advantages and safety of our Rocky Mountain health resorts in pulmonary cases, and those with inherited or acquired tendencies to the disease. My personal knowledge of these resorts has been attained by a residence of eight years in Colorado Springs with occasional visits to other sections of the State. I will confine my observations chiefly to my resident city; what we may say of one resort will apply to all in this region with a few minor modifications.

Colorado Springs is located on a plateau 6,000 feet above sea level. The base of Pike's Peak is six miles directly to the west. Here this eternal sentinel rears its summit 8,134 feet above the level of the city. The mountain ranges extend in a north-easterly and south-easterly direction from the peak at an elevation of 4,000 to 5,000 feet above the city. To the north and northeast we have the land rising to an elevation of 1,000 feet higher than our city.

From a study of our surroundings we see that Colorado Springs is in a more or less protected valley open to the south and south-east where we have the great plains that gradually descend to the Mississippi. This arrangement of mountains and plains causes a diurnal interchange of atmosphere which is very acceptable on a summer's day. The protection of mountains and highlands serves to control the snowfall and rainfall in our vicinity and tempers the storm to a great extent.

The plateau, on which we are located, has a gradual descent from north to south through the city, insuring the best of drainage. The soil in the main part of the city is open and porous. On the surface it is sandy with a slight admixture of alluvial deposit. Below it is gravel for seventy feet to bed rock. To the east and west of the main or central part of the city the surface soil is more or less adobe.

The city is well sewered. Large appropriations have been made in recent years and the extension of the sewers has kept pace with the growth of the city. No cesspools are allowed to be constructed and all sewage is conducted well beyond the city limits.

The plumbing of our residences is under the control of city ordinances, and is put in under the supervision of an efficient plumbing inspector.

The residence portion of our city is built mostly of wood; this permits of varied architectural designs which are pleasing to the eye. Land being plentiful when the city was laid out, we have very wide streets and avenues. The lots are of good size, hence there is no crowding up of buildings. This insures good air, good ventilation and an abundance of sunlight. The water supply is from two sources. That for the lawns is conveyed in open ditches. It comes from the mountain streams and runs in the ditch boxes from April to October. The drinking water comes from a series of mountain reservoirs covering 320 acres. The lowest of these reservoirs, Lake Moraine, is 10,278 feet above sea level. The water is conveyed to the city through pipe lines. I am indebted to Dr. G. B. Webb for the following bacteriological examination of our water supply, made during 1897, for the Board of Health:

Average for the week ending August 21st, 76 colonies per cubic centimeter.

August 28th, 97 colonies per cubic centimeter.

September 4th, 70 colonies per cubic centimeter.

September 11th, 110 colonies per cubic centimeter.

Lake Moraine showed 48 colonies per cubic centimeter. From these examinations it appears that our drinking water is far above the average in purity. Further it must be remembered that these examinations were made at the time of the year when our water is supposed to be at its most contaminated condition.. It is soft, clear and sparkling.

Let us for a time study the meteorological conditions existing in this region. We have a government meteorological station located in our city. It is under the control of Prof. P. E. Doudna, to whom I am indebted for the following:

TEMPERATURE CHART.

	1895			1896			1897			Mean Temp. 3 yrs.	Mean Temp. 18 yrs.
	MAX.	MIN.	MEAN	MAX.	MIN.	MEAN	MAX.	MIN.	MEAN		
January ..	39.4	16.1	27 7	48.2	21.8	35 0	37.7	13.2	25.5	29.4	26.5
February .	36.7	12.4	24.5	45.1	20.6	32.9	39.7	17.9	28 8	28.7	30.0
March	46.9	24 9	35.9	45.7	23.0	34 3	45.7	23.6	34 6	34.9	37.3
April	60.3	32.3	46.6	61 6	34.4	48.0	55.9	32.4	44.2	46.2	44.8
May	64.0	40.3	52.1	69.6	42 7	56.1	67 8	43.7	53.7	54.6	53.8
June	71.6	46.9	58 3	79 5	49.3	64 4	76.1	48.0	62 1	61 9	63.4
July	74.9	51 9	63.4	81 0	55.7	68 4	80.5	52.2	66.4	66.1	68.8
August	77.8	53.1	65.5	80 0	54 0	67.0	77.8	53.1	65 5	66.0	68.3
September	77.5	47.1	62.3	69.4	45.9	57.7	75.4	49.4	62.4	60.8	68 9
October ...	60 4	32 6	47 0	59.9	35 0	47.5	61.2	35.9	48.6	47.7	48.1
November	47.6	22.6	35.1	46 7	21 2	33 9	53.1	27.2	40.1	36 4	36 2
December	40.5	16.5	28 5	50 4	23 2	56.8	40 3	15.1	27.7	31.0	30 3

The observations in the foregoing table were made at 6 a. m., 12 m. and 6 p. m. They do not always represent the lowest minimum temperature, but include the temperatures interesting to the health seeker. It will be noted that the temperature varies but little from year to year during the same month, and the seasons are about the same. The daily variations are often quite marked. The summers are quite cool. It will be noted that the highest temperature recorded during the summer of 1895 was 77.5 degrees; in 1896, 81 degrees, and in 1897, 80.5 degrees. These are shade temperatures. The nights are always cool during the summer.

PRECIPITATION, HUMIDITY AND CLOUDINESS.

	PRECIPITATION IN INCHES.					Av. Daily Humidity			CLOUDINESS.		
	1895	1896	1897	Av. 3 yrs.	Av. 18 yrs.	1895	1896	1897	1895	1896	1897
January ..	0 13	0.13	0 10	0 12	0.18	54.3	60.0	68.5	6 19	6 10 12	9 22 7 2
February .	0.71	0.13	1.02	0 62	0.29	60 3	62.5	73.0	10 18	5 16 6	7 12 9 7
March	0.40	2 57	0 48	1.15	0 67	52.0	73 0	57.5	19 7	5 6 8	17 16 8 7
April	0.60	0.40	0.54	0.57	1.38	53 3	51 0	59 5			
May .	2.70	0 81	1 27	1.59	2 33	49.0	45.0	64.5	14 9 8	11 11	9 10 11 10
June	4 56	1.37	0 80	2 24	1.68	64.3	51.0	55.0	12 13 5	9 10 11	10 10 10
July	3 79	3 10	3 84	3 41	3.20	59 6	59 0	49 0	10 11 10	9 14 8 16	8 7
August	1.89	2.43	2 55	2.29	2 28	59.0	60.0	64.0	10 14 7	9 14 8 18	9 4
September	0.15	2.58	0.74	1.16	1.08	46 0	71.0	56.0	16 9 5	10 8 12 14	8 8
October . .	1.66	0.36	0.54	0.85	0.60	54 6	71.0	58.0	21 6 4	14 6 11 18	6 7
November	0.32	0 08	0.19	0.18	0 31	54 3	59.0	59.0	16 11 3	16 12 2 21	5 4
December .	0.18	0.07	0.06	0 10	0.27	65.3	49.5	67 5	16 8 7 20	6 5 21	3 7

Explanation—

Clear Sky, .0— .3 covered.
Part Cloudy, .4— .7 covered.
Cloudy Sky, .7—1.0 covered.
Average precipitation for the past eighteen years, 14.27 inches.
Number of clear days and part cloudy in 1895, 295.
Number of clear days and part cloudy in 1896, 263.
Number of clear days and part cloudy in 1897, 284.

The table shows at a glance which are the very dry months. Our rainy season commences in May and ends with August. Exceptionally we have a heavy rain earlier in the spring, (March, '96) or later in the fall (September, '96, October, '95). More than three-fourths of the rain falls in one-third of the year. It does not follow that the summer months are cloudy and damp, even though rains are frequent. Note the proportion of days on which the sun shone the greater part of the day during the rainy season. Again, owing to the porosity of the soil and sub-soil the water does not

long remain on the surface and the invalid is out in a very short
time after a hard shower. The average daily humidity will show
the relative quantity of moisture in our atmosphere and is in contrast with our sister states at sea level.

The total number of clear days is very large each year. It must
be remembered that on many of the days reported as cloudy the
sun shone a small portion of the time.

The Health Department of our city is under the control of a
Health Officer. I am indebted to the recent Health Officer, Dr.
B. B. Grover, for the following vital statistics:

	1894	1895	1896	1897
Death rate, per 1,000	13.86	15.44	17.75	13.00
Death rate, per 1,000, excluding consump- tion contracted elsewhere..............	7 02	8 22	12.85	8.22
Consumption contracted in Colorado.......	0	2.	0.	2.

It is very readily seen that the death rate per 1,000 is greatly
increased by the coming to our city of consumptive patients. Hence
it is but right that we should count this class out when looking into
the health of Colorado Springs.

The disinfection of rooms or dwellings is required after all contagious diseases and is under the guidance and control of the
Health Officer, who is well equipped with modern means of disinfection. Disinfection of rooms where advanced tuberculous patients
have lived or died is required by the Health Officer and performed
by him when request is made. One of our best hotels makes it
a practice to disinfect all rooms vacated by anyone not in good
health during their occupancy.

The Health Department flushes the gutters frequently on the
main thoroughfares and there is an ordinance prohibiting expec-
torating on the side-walks and in public conveyances. All paved
walks are required to be washed daily during the summer months.

All food supplies are under strict inspection and are not allowed
to be exposed for sale until examined by the food inspector.

To be contented the invalid has to be entertained. In this matter
we are not excelled by any resort in the West. The natural scenic
environments of Colorado Springs are not surpassed by those of any
place. Nature has been most lavish in her work. We have the
Garden of the Gods, Pike's Peak, Cheyenne Canons with the Seven
Falls, Engleman and Williams Canons, Ute Pass with Rainbow
Falls, and the wonderful, world-renowned springs at Manitou. All
these places are within pleasant drives of our city and will furnish

entertainment for many months. Most of these places are also reached by the electric car lines.

Besides these physical features afforded by nature we boast a number of clubs, race tracks, golf links and other entertainments. We have good hotels and numerous boarding houses.

Notwithstanding all these things we do not have perfection at all times in our climate. The spring winds (during February, March and April) are at times, and particularly to some individuals, quite disagreeable. The summer rains, although quite inconvenient to the tourist and oftimes to the invalid, are welcomed by the resident population. The sudden changes in the temperature in the winter are often quite marked. Owing to the very dry atmosphere during the winter months the changes are noticed but little in the patient's condition.

The summer months are cool and pleasant. The direct rays of the sun are quite warm but one can always be comfortable in the shade. The nights are never sultry and one can always sleep well. The want of humidity in the atmosphere makes the dew point low hence we have but few mornings that the invalid has to remain in doors on account of dews. The arrangement of mountains and plains makes a diurnal interchange of air that is very agreeable.

Now, what of all these facts compiled from various sources? Why are they given? I have been thus explicit to show that we are endowed by nature and the art of man as a great sanitarium. It is not my purpose to try and prove that our climate is especially adapted to the treatment of pulmonary cases. This fact is conceded by all who have made them a study.

The altitude, the location, the protection by the mountains, the character of the soil, the great amount of sunshine and the pure water supply, are essential elements on nature's part for a first-class health resort.

The care in protecting our water supply from contamination, the supplying of an abundance of water to each household, the care in putting in plumbing and sewerage, the cleansing of our sidewalks and gutters, the complete health ordinances of our Board of Health carried out by an efficient executive officer, together with our broad streets and large lawns permitting the sunlight to enter our homes, are precautions on the part of man that will insure the greatest safety to the health of our inhabitants.

Have all these things produced any results? We answer in the affirmative. To prove our position we will have to make a few comparisons. This is not always a pleasant thing to have done, but we will ask your tolerance for a short time.

The average death rate per 1,000 population (excluding consumption contracted elsewhere, and it would not be just to include these when rating the health of this community) for the past four years is 9.08. Death rate in the whole United States is 13.98 per 1,000; in New York City, 28.63 per 1,000; in Chicago, 21.06 per 1,000;; in Boston, 24.79 per 1,000 (Eleventh Census Report, 1890). We see that the rate in our city is one-third less than that of the whole United States and two and more times less than in the larger cities. So much for the general health.

What can we say of the danger of contracting tuberculosis in Colorado Springs? In the past four years there have been four cases reported as having died of consumption contracted in Colorado Springs. During this time we have had an average population of 18,000. This would give the death rate from consumption of .055 to 1,000 population. ' Compare this with other sections of the country. The death rate from consumption in the United States is 1.642 per 1,000; in Peoria, Ill., (the city nearest to my former patient) is 2. to 1,000; in Boston, 3.95 to 1,000; in New York, 3.87 to 1,000; in Arizona, natives, .5 to 1,000; in Colorado, natives, .41 to 1,000. (Eleventh census 1890. It is but fair to state that this rate has been diminished slightly in some of the eastern cities of recent years.)

We would deduce from this comparison that the lady's chances of contracting tuberculosis are 37 times greater in her home in Illinois than they would be in Colorado Springs.

The immunity of the residents of Colorado Springs from tuberculosis is rather remarkable when we consider that the majority of the families here have come to Colorado for the health of some member of the family. Very often, I will say in the majority of instances, this member of the family is the father or mother. We would naturally suppose that a population made up of these family predispositions, would furnish many examples of the disease. But such is not the case. We cannot assert that our climate will prevent one from becoming inoculated with tuberculosis. when proper precautions are not taken. The cases reported during 1897 were both due to carelessness. The hygienic surroundings were poor, the food was scanty, the tendencies were all that could be inherited, and under these conditions we may expect the disease to be propagated.

With due regard to the rules of hygiene and general health we will say that the dangers of contracting tuberculosis in Colorado Springs are as little as anywhere else, and many times less than in the central and eastern states. We feel that in our pure, dry air and bright sunshine we have germ destroyers that are not equalled by any other natural parasiticide in the world.

What has been said of Colorado Springs as a health resort can be applied, in all essential points, to the other cities of the Rocky Mountain region.

Denver is a city excelled by none in the west. It has the advantage of being a larger city and offers greater inducements to those wanting to engage in mercantile pursuits. It is lower (elevation 5,280 feet,) and this in turn is often a material advantage. To those liking a city life with its greater line of amusements it is to be preferred.

Pueblo is farther out on the plains than these cities and is quite hot during the summer months. The altitude is not so great and many patients do well there who do not thrive at a greater altitude.

Canon City is well protected from the winter winds, and is endowed with soda springs, hot and cold, and garners rich horticultural products.

Manitou is really a part of Colorado Springs as far as climate is concerned and is a very popular resort during the summer months. (Manitou is connected by electric street car system and by two steam car lines with Colorado Springs,—about five miles distant.—Editor.)

If one delights in mountain scenery he will find Estes Park, Woodland Park, Green Mountain Falls, Cascade and other very pleasant places in which spend the hot summer months. The elevation is greater and scenery all that any mountain region could boast.

Excerpts from "The Western Medical ....and Surgical Gazette."

I. DISEASES OF CHILDREN IN COLORADO.

By H. B. Whitney, M. D., Denevr, Colo.

Professor of Medicine in the University of Denver, Visiting Physician Denver and Arapahoe County Hospital.

In the first place it may be unhesitatingly affirmed that Colorado infants are unusually exempt from the more serious acute diseases of the gastro-intestinal canal.

Here lies the crucial point of the whole matter. Our dry climate is primarily unfavorable to fermentation and putrefactive processes; a moderate thermometric range during the summer months still further favors the preservation of milk; and, most important of all, the milk is delivered to the consumer within twelve, and often within six hours of the time of milking.

Our dairies are all within a short distance of the city. Many of them are kept in excellent hygienic condition, and in general, an excellent quality of milk is furnished to even the poorer parts of the city. Add to these factors the absence of all crowding into densely populated districts and large tenement houses, and no further explanation is required. While, therefore, Colorado can offer no guarantee against the ordinary dyspeptic disturbances which will ever be the lot of infants prematurely deprived of the mother's breast, we can nevertheless present unequalled inducements to the hand-fed baby.

We can positively assure him that his direst enemy, cholera infantum, is rarely seen in these parts; personally I can recall but two cases of genuine cholera infantum in a practice of eleven years.

The influence of the Colorado climate upon pulmonary tuberculosis is too well known to need further emphasis here. I cannot remember ever to have seen a case in a child under ten years; and though this is not the place for discussion of the question of heredity, I would here express my conviction that the future of the children of tuberculous parents, and the infinitely better chances of escape which the Rocky Mountain region affords, have been too little regarded by eastern pedriatricists.

There is a prevalent impression among Eastern physicians that acute pneumonias are particularly dangerous at and above an altitude of 5,000 feet.

There is, indeed, some basis for this belief, in that pneumonia at Leadville, for example, (10,000) is, from all I can learn, an unusually fatal affection. However that may be, and whatever may be the cause, (possibly other than altitude, in a population consisting largely of miners,) I am certain that it is not true of Denver. Some six years ago I reported 58 cases of acute lobar pneumonia which had been under my personal care during the previous winter. Though most of these were adults, among whom the mortality is confessedly larger than in children, there was a total of but 13 deaths; and of these nine were grouped together and unquestionably the result of the prevailing epidemic of grippe.

The altitude of Denver, is, I believe, widely credited with exercising an unfavorable influence upon the nervous system. It is thought to foster and maintain a high degree of nervous tension, and to favor the development of a great many functional disorders. I have come to regard the belief in this influence as greatly exaggerated. Among adults, especially women, it may be very seriously questioned whether much of the "nervousness" complained of is not the result of suggestion and the prevalent notion that in such a dry and elevated region, the nerves also must necessarily become dry and brittle. Again, this idea is an especially attractive and seductive one to that large class of people who like to feel that duty to themselves demands a yearly trip to the seashore.

Chorea may be somewhat more prevalent, due to the greater frequency of rheumatism, but this disorder stands alone. Convulsions, tetany, headaches, palpitations, hysteria, are probably as common in Colorado as elsewhere, but no more so. And in general it may be confidently affirmed that Colorado children will develop into as stable adult nervous organisms as those of other regions.

In conclusion I may state my firm conviction that Denver and other similarly situated Colorado regions are unusually favored localities for child growth and development.

II. PULMONARY HEMORRHAGES IN COLORADO.

.

By S. G. Bonney, A. M., M. D., Denver, Colo.

Professor of Medicine, University of Denver, Visiting Physician,
St. Luke's Hospital.

An analysis is made of 350 recorded cases of pulmonary tuberculosis, selected from private practice, and subjected to continuous observation. No consideration is here given to other than the relation of the Colorado Springs climate to pulmonary hemorrhages. From statistical data, it would seem rational to conclude:

1. That the susceptibility to hemorrhage in pulmonary invalids, is decidedly greater in those with nervous than with phlegmatic temperaments.

2. That hemorrhagic cases in general, constituting about one-half the entire number, do rather better in Colorado than the non-hemorrhagic.

3. That those cases with distinctly hemorrhagic onset, in the absence of pronounced symptoms, or existence of physical signs, respond more than all others to the favorable influences of the climate, presumably on account of the early diagnosis secured and the more prompt recourse to climatic change.

4. That in those with previous hemorrhages the proportion of recurrences in Colorado is small, but the ultimate results less satisfactory.

5. That not far from one in ten or twelve may be expected to have a primary hemorrhage in Colorado, those belonging to this class furnishing the smallest percentage of improvement.

6. That recurrences, shortly after arrival, are more likely to ensue in those cases with hemorrhage within one month before coming to Colorado, the ultimate prognosis, however, being by no means necessarily unfavorable.

7. That hemorrhages occurring after a prolonged residence in Colorado are usually more serious and attended more frequently with unfortunate results.

8. That no definite relation exists between the development of the hemorrhage, and either the extent of pulmonary involvement or the degree of activity of the tubercular process, the larger number of those before arrival occurring during comparatively slight inactive infection, and nearly half of those in Colorado taking place in the course of pronounced improvement.

9. That, as is well known, the existence of moderately extensive cavity formation predisposes to the tendency to hemorrhages, although not more so in Colorado than elsewhere.

10. That even copious hemorrhages, resulting from rupture of small pulmonary aneurisms, although always of serious moment, and possibly more frequent in Colorado than at lower elevations, are not necessarily associated with a uniformly unfavorable prognosis.

11. That the avoidance of pulmonary hemorrhage in Colorado demands competent, continuous medical supervision, and strict compliance with detailed instructions with reference to rest and mode of life.

III. A PRELIMINARY COMPARISON OF THE METHODS AND RESULTS OF OPERATIVE SURGERY AT THE SEA LEVEL (NEW YORK) AND IN PLACES OF HIGH ALTITUDE (DENVER).

By Charles A. Powers, M. D., Denver, Colo.

Professor of Surgery in the University of Denver; Surgeon to St. Luke's Hospital and to the Arapahoe County Hospital.

---

1. Operative surgery in dry climates, having an altitude of one mile, or thereabout, is to be pursued on the same general lines which govern it at the sea level. However,

2. Care must be exercised in subjecting those recently from a low altitude to severe or prolonged surgical procedure, especially if the patient be a pulmonary invalid or if he exhibit cardiac weakness; and

3. It would seem that those who are thoroughly acclimated bear operation rather better when at home than when they go to tidewater, and this again is particularly true of patients afflicted with pulmonary tuberculosis.

4. Ether must be employed with greater caution, and is more of an irritant to the respiratory mucous membrane. Chloroform may find wider employment than at the sea level.

5. The loss of blood seems to be rather less in the high, dry climate, possibly excepting cases in which the operative field is the seat of chronic inflammation.

6. Shock, also, seems to be less pronounced, patients rally rather more quickly after operation. In the tuberculous this feature seems to be marked.

7. Aseptic wound management must be the same in all regions. Infection, when it occurs, doubtless makes less progress in a dry atmosphere than in one containing a greater degree of moisture.

8. It is believed that accumulated statistics will show that operations for surgical tuberculosis are attended by a greater permanency of healing in the high altitudes, and that patients presenting such lesions, but whose lungs are yet free, do all possible to ward off pulmonary invasion by taking up their abode in such a climate as that of Colorado.

IV. NERVOUSNESS IN RELATION TO ALTITUDES.

By Howell T. Pershing, M. D., Denver, Colo.

As is well known, there is a very general belief, held by both the physicians and laity of Colorado, that functional nervous disorders are more common here than elsewhere and that the altitude is the cause of it. Like most popular beliefs it is not well defined, being held at one time or another as to all forms of functional nervous disease, but as far as I can ascertain, it is applied most often to neurasthenia and hysteria. Leaving aside for a moment the question of the truth or falsit·· of this belief, I am convinced that its prevalence amongst nervous invalids is often an obstacle to recovery. Hysterical patients, always ready to respond to the suggestion of a bad feeling, are likely to associate any they may chance to have with the altitude and so expect it to return unless a change of climate is made. Neurasthenic patients, too, are often highly suggestible and the depressing idea of being in an unfavorable climate often tends to prolong the disease if it does not lead to the great sacrifices of money and position which are often involved in a change of residence. It is important then to examine the evidence for the beliefs in order to be certain whether it is really sufficient.

For the past nine years I have been practising in Denver as a neurologist, seeing patients from various parts of the state, and a very large proportion of my work has been the treatment of neurasthenia and hysteria. During this time I have carefully looked for some tangible evidence that nervousness is caused or made harder to manage by any physical climate, but have failed to find any except the mere fact that such a belief is held by able men. Not only do the reasons commonly given in its support seem fallacious to me, but my own experience has led me to form a diametrically opposite view, namely, that the physical effects of Colorado climate exercise a favorable influence on most nervous patients. Dr. H. B. Whitney tells me that he does not find the nervous disorders of children to be either more frequent or more severe here than at lower altitudes, and Dr. Solly, in his Medical Climatology, speaks of the Colorado climate as having a favorable influence in many cases of neurasthenia.*

*The Climatologist, Vol. i.

This question cannot be settled directly by an appeal to statistics, the diseases not being fatal and very few physicians keeping any accurate record of them. Some years ago Dr. Eskridge made a study of the relative frequency and duration of chorea in Colorado based upon answers from representative physicians throughout the state to letters of inquiry in addition to his own experience. The conclusion he reached was that chorea was comparatively infrequent and of short duration in Denver, and that the fear of a serious unfavorable influence at higher altitudes is not justified by facts. I heartily concur in this conclusion and have often thought of making similar inquiries as to hysteria and neurasthenia, but have not been able to formulate a plan that promises accurate results. There are, nevertheless, certain arguments, which to my mind, afford a strong support to the opinion I have formed from my own experience. In presenting these, for the sake of clearness and simplicity, I shall refer to neurasthenia alone because climatic conditions could be a cause of hysteria, if at all, only by creating a predisposing neurasthenia.

All who have made a special study of neurasthenia agree that it is a state of irritable weakness of the nerve centers, depending upon the insufficiency of their nutritive processes to repair the exhaustion caused by over-use or by the depressing effects of auto-intoxication. In the treatment of neurasthenia, accordingly, we have three cardinal aims; to improve nutrition, to secure rest and recreation, and to prevent auto-intoxication. It does not seem to me that these aims are at all interfered with by the Colorado climate. The wonderfully favorable effect of the climate upon pulmonary tuberculosis is not attributed by the physicians who have most to do with this disease to any local effect of the rarefied air upon the lungs, but to an improvement in the nutrition of the body as a whole

If it were not so, other forms of tubercular disease would be especially rife here, on account of the large number of tubercular patients who have made Colorado their permanent residence, yet they seem to be comparatively rare. Dr. George B. Packard, who has had good opportunities of observing diseases of the bones and joints in New York and in Denver, tells me that tubercular bone disease seems to him to be remarkably infrequent here. On a priori grounds it is only reasonable to infer that the climatic influence which strengthens the resistance of the whole body to tuberculosis also acts favorably on the nervous system, and in support of this inference I am able to adduce some clinical evidence. Dr. S. G. Bonney has kept a record of the nervous complications in his pulmonary cases and he finds not only that consumptives with complicating neurasthenia do nearly as well as the average but that the nervousness generally improves at the same time as the pulmonary lesions.

That the blood contains a higher average of haemoglobin as well as a greater number of red corpuscles in high altitude is well known and it has been shown that this is not due, as one might at first suspect, to an excessive loss of water by the body, but to an actual increase of haemoglobin in proportion to the body weight. As we are generally anxious to enrich the blood of neurasthenics it is not easy to regard this tendency to an increase in the haemoglobin as anything else than favorable.

As to recreation, our climate, inviting to out-door sports the year around, is a decidedly favorable one. Possibly it invites some persons to an excessive activity, but this is easily guarded against. An agreeable change in the mode of activity is usually more desirable than absolute rest, and if rest rather than recreation is essential I believe it can be secured in Colorado as well as elsewhere.

It must be admitted that the uric acid diathesis, which is an important factor in many cases of neurasthenia, is very frequent in Colorado, but it is certainly very frequent elsewhere. I know of no data by which its relative frequency in different localities can be determined, but general impressions seem to indicate that, like its special representatives, rheumatism and gout, it is most prevalent in cool, moist climates, such as that of the great lakes or northern coasts of the United States. It may be asked how the general belief as to the bad effect of the Colorado climate on nervous persons could have arisen if not well founded. I suppose it arose from observation of the very startling effect which rapid change to a high altitude sometimes causes. In its extreme form this effect is known as mountain sickness and in its milder form is generally felt for a short time on first coming from sea level to even such an altitude as that of Denver or Colorado Springs. It was very natural to suppose that such symptoms of nervous, circulatory and respiratory derangement must indicate some continuous bad influence of the climate. I am quite sure, however, that these symptoms are in the great majority of persons very transient; that as the tension of the fluids of the body become equal to that of the atmosphere and as the muscles of respiration adapt themselves to their changed conditions and the oxygen-carrying power of the blood increases the symptoms absolutely vanish. Whymfer and his companions, previously accustomed to the more moderate elevation of the Alps, on reaching an altitude in the Andes of between 16,000 and 17,000 feet suffered extremely from mountain sickness, but recovered in a few days and had no return of the symptoms, although they afterwards climbed to a summit more than 20,000 feet in height.

Another reason for the general belief may be the idea that neurasthenia, being an irritable state, requires sedative drugs, such as bromides, and hence a sedative climate, while the Colorado climate is generally classed as stimulating. The fact is, however, that the weakness of neurasthenia demands treatment rather than the irritability, which is secondary, and that bromides continuously administered are decidedly harmful, while the strychnia does good. Therefore, if the effect of drugs is a reliable indication, for the great majority of neurasthenic patients a bracing climate is decidedly preferable.

However it may have originally been suggested, there is no difficulty in understanding how the idea of an adverse climatic influence has since been perpetuated.

Neurasthenia is a difficult disease to handle, continually baffling even the most skillful physician who attempts to treat it symptomatically, as he would many other diseases, without a careful and sympathetic study of this peculiar class of patients and their apparently lawless mental vagaries. It is then very natural for a physician who has patiently tried various remedies without success to suppose that there is some unaccountable adverse influence at work and to fall in with the prevalent view as to the effects of the altitude. So patients are often told that they must go to another altitude.

Of course those who go away reap the benefit of the rest, recreation and change of scene incident to the trip, in addition to the very valuable mental effect of feeling that they now have a sovereign remedy. This, however, does not prove that a high altitude had anything to do with their symptoms for the same class of patients residing at sea level derives just as much benefit from a vacation in Colorado, and Denver patients of the same class do very well in the higher regions of Estes Park and Middle Park, provided they stay long enough and have a good time.

As to the effect of extremely high altitudes I am not prepared to say anything definite. Of course there must be a limit beyond which efficient compensation for the thinness of the air can not take place, but I see no reason to suppose that this limit has been reached in Colorado.

Some Notes.

By J. T. Estill, M. D., Colorado Springs, Colo.

The climate of Colorado is especially useful in alleviating and curing the various forms of pulmonary troubles, it at the same time exerts a very beneficial influence upon most diseases. My observations upon forty-five cases of typhoid fever in the St. Francis hospital convince me, that while the duration of the disease is not materially lessened, the symptoms are much milder than in lower altitudes with malarial influences. It would be interesting to go into details of such cases if space would allow, but let it be sufficient to state that the atmosphere being absolutely free from malaria, the patient, after the fever subsides, recuperates very rapidly and the recovery is complete.

Again, observation teaches us that the cases of contagious disease are much milder and less complicated in Colorado than in Eastern localities, where malarial influences exert such baneful effects by bringing about serious complications.

The rarity of infection and the prompt and complete recovery in labor cases is evident to every accoucheur; and the same is true in all kinds of surgical cases; which betterment must, for the most part, be attributed to the purity of this atmosphere.

It seems unnecessary to state that for teething children and children of scrofulous diathesis suffering from anaemia and indigestion, the invigorating influence of this mountain air acts like a charm.

Ibealtb IResorts for
...Xung Troubles.

A LETTER

Containing Personal Experiences, Published in the New York
Tribune of May 22, 1887, and Notes
Appended in 1898.

BY LOUIS R. EHRICH.

Colorado Springs, Colo., May 8.

The great prevalence of lung disease, my conviction that the disease can be arrested and in many cases cured by the proper climatic influences, and, further, my knowledge of the difficulty of obtaining unprejudiced information as to the character of climates—all these considerations have induced me to publish the following record of my experience as a lung patient.

I was a merchant in New York City. Like my more prominent fellow-merchants of that mad metropolis, I was consumed with a wild ambition, not only to develop my business to vast proportions, but also to outdistance all competitors. My partners and I worked with intense energy. We condensed the work of a month into a week. We centered our whole life in our business. We prospered rapidly, but increased prosperity only added fuel to our ambition.

The question of health never entered into my calculation. I allowed myself no vacation—never realized the need of a rest. For several years my face had worn that pale, haggard expression which might be called the New York business man's complexion; but I experienced no indications of weakness or ill-health. One morning in August, 1878, I awoke with a strange, warm, soft feeling in my throat. It was a hemorrhage from the right lung. Then the overwork of years declared itself, my nervous force was completely exhausted, and a violent fever robbed me of flesh and strength.

"Complete change," the doctors said, "Europe, a year's rest!" I asked, "Where shall the year be spent?" My own physician frankly admitted that he knew little about European climates; so we consulted one of the great authorities. The authority advised that I spend the winter in Rome. Let me say right here that, in my opinion, the winter climate of Rome is one of the worst in Europe for a consumptive, and, further, that this first consultation proved to me what my many subsequent consultations have proved more strongly, namely, that American physicians (and European physicians, for that matter,) know very little about climates. A successful American physician is just as busy in his business as I was in mine. He may read reports of physicians, who naturally are inclined to extol the climate of their own locality, but he knows nothing on the subject from personal experience, and personal experience is the only safe guide in the question of judging climates.

To Europe I went. On the road to Marseilles, whence I intended to take steamer for Rome (via Civita Vecchia), I fell into talk with an Englishman, who informed me that the climate of Nice and Mentone was infinitely preferable to that of Rome. As I was only a few hours' travel from Nice, I resolved to go there as an experiment. Never shall I forget my first day at Nice! Coming from the snow and piercing damp of Paris to the soft, balmy air of the Riviera, with its semi-tropical vegetation, its lovely walks and drives, its enchanting outlook on the deep blue Mediterranean, it seemed to me as if I had been transported to paradise. That winter I spent on the Riviera, principally at Mentone. Finally, on March 1, much against the advice of friends, I started for Rome. I spent seven weeks in the Eternal City, subsequently going to Sorrento, Florence and Venice, but at none of these places did I find, even late in the spring, the weather as mild and sunny as it had been at Nice and Mentone in midwinter. About the middle of June I arrived at Munich and consulted Professor Buhl (at that time a great South German medical authority) as to where I should spend the summer. I had heard a great deal of Davos, Switzerland, and wanted to go there. Professor Buhl, however, informed me with an air of wisdom that the altitude of Davos (5,000 feet) was provocative of hemorrhage, and sent me first to Soden, a pleasant little watering place near Frankfort-on-the-Main, and later to Heiden, an insignificant resort near Lake Constance, where I felt so miserably that I was glad to leave it. The summer over, physicians pronounced me "almost well." Consumptive reader, never let the phrase "almost well" impose upon you! As a Scotch physician, to whom I repeated the expression, truthfully said: "It is like saying that there is only a very small spark still alight in the powder magazine. That tiny spark may produce death and destruction. No rational man ought to be satisfied until that last spark has been thoroughly stamped out."

I returned to New York in October and remained there all winter. Three hours of every morning I gave up to business, and the afternoons I devoted to horseback riding. I seemed to improve constantly, so that when, the following June, I had my lungs examined by the late Dr. Austin Flint, he pronounced me perfectly well. To make assurance doubly sure I spent that summer camping out in the Adirondack mountains. I continued to gain in weight and strength. In the middle of August came one of those drenching rains common to the Adirondack region. It rained three successive days, soaked the camp and surroundings, and lowered the temperature very considerably. I caught a severe cold, which I could not throw off in the mountains, and which still clung to me when I reached New York in September. Consumptives, give heed! I looked the picture of health, weighed twenty pounds more than before I was first taken sick, and only three months before Dr. Flint had pronounced me perfectly well. I began to devote more time to business, giving up only part of the afternoon to horseback riding. Five weeks had scarcely passed when, riding in Central Park, I began to cough violently, expectorated blood, and at once heard in my chest that dreadful crunching sound which betokens a hemorrhage. Scarcely had I reached home and bed before a violent hemorrhage declared itself. The hemorrhages occurred again and again, and it was six months before I left my room. I went to Aiken, South Carolina, for six weeks. It did me no good. The summer I passed at the Mountain House, Cornwall-on-the-Hudson, where my health steadily improved. In the fall I went to Europe. The first three years I spent at the following places: Three winters at Mentone, two spring seasons in Italy, one spring at Merau in the Tyrol, two summers at Reichenhall, Bavaria, one summer in Engelberg, Switzerland. I improved somewhat all the time, but, altogether, very inconsiderably.

The conviction finally forced itself upon me that there was no curative quality for lung trouble in the air of the Riviera. It is a delightful place to live (barring cholera and earthquakes), and for consumptives whose cases are extreme, who have high fever and little vitality, it probably is a very good place to spend the winter. In my own case, however, it produced no benefits, so I determined, against the advice of several physicians, to try higher altitudes. The summer of 1884 I ventured to spend at Saint Moritz (elevation 6,000 feet) and the following winter, from September to April, at Davos, Switzerland. Davos is so peculiar in its climate and surroundings, it has gained so great a reputation as a resort for consumptives, that an extended description of it is warranted.

Davos lies in a well sheltered valley, about half a mile wide and two miles long; altitude 4,800 feet above sea level. It is a village of hotels built on the side of the mountain, so as to escape the draught of the valley below. The snow generally falls there in October, and the ground remains snow-covered until the middle of April. The nights are very cold; the days, so long as the sun shines into the valley, very warm. During the months of January and February I ate my lunch on a veranda in the open air, the awning drawn overhead to shield us from the sun, whereas five feet from where we sat the snow lay three feet deep. Back of the hotels the mountain rises several thousand feet. For a thousand feet up, a footpath, leading to an abandoned hut called the Schatz-Alp, is thoroughly kept in order by the municipality and forms the principal walk of the patients.

The motto of Davos as regards climate and mode of life is "Harden yourself!" The more hardy patients walk a great deal, climb up to the Schatz-Alp every day, and are out in all weather. All the invalids sleep with their windows wide open. Many skate and toboggan. Be it remarked that during the winter one seldom takes cold at Davos. Let me sum up the advantages and disadvantages of this celebrated resort:

Advantages:

1. Altitude of nearly 5,000 feet. The lungs get more exercise and increased exercise gives them increased elasticity and strength.

2. The air is invigorating, dry and cold, and yet warm enough during sunshine to allow delicate patients to sit out of doors.

3. There is no dust. The snow prevents this.

4. There is no cloudy, foggy weather. Except when snow falls the days are all sunny.

5. There is little wind, very little up where the hotels are situated.

6. The hotels are very well managed (especially Kurhaus Holsboer), and go far toward supplying home comfort.

Disadvantages:

1. Davos is one great hospital and nothing else. All who go there go for their health only.

2. The patient is penned up in a little snow-covered valley. His walks are limited to the main street or to the climb up the Schatz-Alp. He is naturally compelled to meet the same consumptive ac-

quaintances a hundred times a day. The patient feels imprisoned. He knows that he cannot go beyond the limits of the diminutive valley without imminent danger. Before the winter is half over the daily sight of the same barren, wintry scene, of the same consumptive faces, produces a strong feeling of ennui. One longs for spring as a prisoner longs for the day of his deliverance.

3. The life is all hotel life. There are no furnished cottages for rent, and families would find it difficult to keep house if there were. The crowding together of consumptives in a hotel, the close contact with very sick invalids, the necessity of constantly breathing consumptive exhalations, the shock which a death in a hotel brings, the incessant mutual inquiry and conversation of the guests about their condition, all this is certainly a great injury.

4. The air is too chilly, even when sun warmed, to allow patients to drive with safety. Skating and tobogganing are too violent for the majority. So there is practically no out-of-door amusement for the very sick.

5. The absence of wind has its objections. Very frequently the smoke rests stationary over the town like a bank of clouds. Wind means natural ventilation, and ventilation is very necessary for a town of consumptives.

6. In the early spring, say from the 15th of March, the snow begins to melt. Sore throats and colds abound. The invalid would like to get away, but he dare not, for it is still too cold in other resorts. The snow melting period is always dangerous in Davos.

7. The topography of Davos is such, and this is a very great disadvantage, that the sun rises very late and sets very early. There are unclouded winter days in Davos when there are barely four and a half hours of sunshine.

8. Hardly any one would think of making Davos a permanent residence. No one could afford to unless he had sufficient means to live without work, or went into the hotel business. There is no other industry.

9. Finally, in case the climate disagrees with a patient it is very difficult and very dangerous to change. To reach the Riviera requires a long and circuitous railroad trip through the St. Gotthard to Milan, Genoa and thence to the Riviera, involving the necessity of spending two or three nights on the road and making five changes of cars.

Now as to results: In my own case Davos had no appreciably beneficial effect, except to make my lungs less sensitive. A very near relative spent three consecutive winters at Davos. He felt better while there, but it effected no cure. Personally I know of no case in which a cure was brought about at Davos. Six of the acquaintances of my Davos winter are dead. None the less, I have no hesitation in saying that, in my opinion, Davos is by far the best curative winter resort in Europe for lung patients.

The spring of 1885 I passed at Baden-Baden. There I received letters from a friend and fellow-invalid who had also tried the European climates, but who, being compelled to return to the United States, had spent the winter of 1884-'85 at Colorado Springs, Colorado. He wrote so warmly in praise of the Colorado climate, and I was so tired of living in Europe that I resolved to follow his example. So after visiting Holland and Belgium during the summer, we returned to New York in the fall. I at once consulted three New York medical celebrities. Number one tried to dissuade me from going to Colorado and endeavored to send me back to Davos. Number two shook his head and seemed to expect dreadful results. Number three very sensibly said: "Go and try it. If it does not agree with you in six weeks go on to Santa Barbara." I must remark that not one of these three celebrities knew anything about the existence of Colorado Springs and that to each of them Colorado meant Denver.

On December 2nd I left New York for Colorado. I went with fear and trembling. Chicago gave me a slight taste of its climatic possibilities in the shape of a medley of wind, hail, snow, sleet and rain. So far as the travel went, my two days' railroad ride from Chicago was a rest and a pleasure, but when I looked out at the straggling, neglected, desolate-looking towns of Nebraska, and thought that possibly Colorado Springs might resemble these, my heart sank within me. I had expected to find Colorado very cold. Judge, then, of my glad surprise when, at 7 in the morning, I stepped out of the cars at Denver on the 7th of December. The sun was pouring down a flood of warm, bright light. The air was very mild, yet there was a light, bracing tone in it which made it a delight to breathe. Every inhalation was like a draught of nectar. I thought of snow-bound Davos and was happy. Three hours later brought us to Colorado Springs. Our friends had secured a furnished house for us. Our expectations were exceedingly modest, so that our astonishment was great when a short drive through wide, beautiful streets brought us to a comfortably furnished home equipped with all modern improvements—bath-room, running water (cold and warm), gas, open fireplaces and steam heater, telephone connection and all.

From the day of my arrival my health began to improve. After now having spent two winters and one summer here, I feel warranted in saying (and my range of observation includes Old and New Mexico, which I have lately visited,) that, taking climate and all other conditions into full consideration, Colorado Springs is the best resort on the face of the globe for an invalid with lung disease.

No climate is absolutely perfect, so I shall first call attention to the only blemish in the climate of Colorado Springs. We have some wind and, at times severe wind, yet the number of days when an invalid is compelled to remain indoors on account of strong wind is not more than the number he is compelled to spend indoors at Davos on account of the falling of snow. Furthermore, if an invalid finds the wind objectionable, he can readily escape it by changing to Manitou Springs (10 minutes by rail), which is even more sheltered than Davos.

Now as to the advantages of Colorado Springs:

1. Its altitude is six thousand feet above sea level. To the north the land rises gradually, thickly wooded, to the height of 7,500 feet. Six miles to the west runs a spur of the Rocky Mountains culminating at Pike's Peak, 14,147 feet high. Thus the city is sheltered to the north and west and is open to the south and east.

2. The sunshine is almost uninterrupted. During the winter there is no rain, no cloudy or foggy weather, and hardly any snow. Snow falls very rarely, and when it falls it disappears quickly and almost miraculously, leaving neither mud nor dampness behind.

3. As the city lies open to the east and the higher mountains to the west are at some distance, the daily duration of the winter sunshine is very great—fully forty per cent. greater than at Davos.

4. The character of the soil is porous. This is a very important advantage. If rain or snow falls in Denver, for example, the result is mud, and mud means continued dampness. There is rarely any mud at Colorado Springs.

5. The invalid is not restricted to hotel life. Boarding houses and furnished houses abound. Housekeeping, owing to the presence of a large number of very superior stores, is made easy. Should the invalid prefer hotel life, he will find the hotels first class, but be it said that no American hotels are so carefully managed as to comfort nor so particular as to ventilation, as are the hotels of the Riviera or of Davos.

6. There is nothing of the hospital character about Colorado Springs. Of its 7,000 inhabitants, many never were sick, and many who once were are now perfectly cured. The invalids are scattered to such an extent, there are so many amusements and points of in-

terest to disperse them, that one never feels the depressing influnce of being in a great consumptive hotel.

7. Amusements are very plentiful. There are few cities in the world that offer such a variety of beautiful rides and drives. Invalids are out riding or driving nearly every day in the year. Many people of wealth and culture reside here, society is pleasant and clubs of all kinds abound—social clubs, reading clubs, musical clubs, fox-hunting clubs, etc., etc. An invalid here has neither time nor disposition to mope.

8. One of the objections I found to Davos and the Riviera was that when spring came the patient was chafing to get away. I do not find this at Colorado Springs. Nor is it necessary. The summer climate is just as healthful and just as exceptional as the winter climate. In fact, the reputation of Colorado summers brings thousands of tourists here every summer. The days are warm, not uncomfortably so, and the nights are always cool enough to make a heavy blanket necessary. Some invalids go up the beautiful near-by mountain parks (8,500 to 10,000 feet high), and live at a farm house or camp out. Some change to Manitou Springs and enjoy witnessing the summer gayety. The majority remain here and are equally benefited.

9. If a patient feels disposed to make a change during the winter, he has a large choice of places which he can visit with safety. He may go to Denver or to any of the towns between Colorado Springs and Poncha Springs inclusive. This belt of territory is all favored with an exceptional climate. On the other hand, if an invalid finds that the climate does not agree with him, he can travel hence to Southern California quickly and comfortably.

10. Families will find here all necessary advantages. They will discover that Colorado Springs combines Eastern comforts and Eastern culture with Western sociability and Western freedom. There are good public and private schools, and there is a well-conducted college offering all the advantages of a scientific and classical education.

11. Most Americans, whether from choice or necessity, want to have some business interests. Colorado Springs is not a great business city, but, owing to the advent of several important railroad lines during the coming year, will improve greatly in this respect. None the less, even at present, cattle ranching, sheep ranching and farming of all kinds offer good returns for investments; many enterprises are continually developed here in which capital will win large profits, and merchants in every line of business are making money. Justice compels me to say that the ideal city, so far as the

combination of healthful climate and business opportunity is concerned, is Denver. It is not nearly so perfect a health resort as Colorado Springs (it has the objections of being a large, busy city, of having an adobe soil, and of being less sheltered), but it is a much better place in which to build up a large business. My advice, therefore, is: "Come here and get well. After you are well, if no business opportunity presents itself here, go to Denver and you can both make money there and keep well at the same time."

12. Every patient when he first learns that his lungs are affected, thinks as I did, namely, that after sufficient rest and change he can safely return to his old home and old occupation. This is a dreadful mistake, and does not realize itself once in a thousand times. Sooner or later (and alas! very often too late), the consumptive invalid stands face to face with the fact that he must make a life change of climate or of occupation, or both. If he has tried Colorado Springs and found that the climate suited his case, he knows that, if necessary to change permanently, he can make his home in a beautiful city, offering all comforts and advantages, and peopled by a highly educated community. In the year and a half that I have lived here many acquaintances have gone away. Some went to California, others to Ashville, N. C., others to Europe, and many to their eastern homes. All have come back, and all with the intention of making this their permanent home. The fact is, that when the glory of this climate becomes known, the exceptional beauty and healthfulness of this city, the remarkable scenery of the surrounding country, the character of its society and educational advantages, and its central location for excursion or travel, many people of wealth, who are not invalids, but who wish to escape the fog, damp, excessive heat and cold of the east, will make this the home of their choice.

13. A great advantage of this climate is that its effect very soon declares itself. It is not necessary to spend four winters here, as I did at Mentone, in order to learn that the climate is not benefiting your case. You soon discover whether the effect is good or bad, and must act accordingly.

For some types of lung trouble this climate is deadly in its effect. It is difficult to particularize these cases, simply because every case of lung disease varies with the invalid. Speaking broadly, invalids with high fever, with rapid waste of tissue and with low vitality, should not come here. None the less, I am assured by physicians that some of those very types of consumption have done remarkably well here.

A word as to results: The only stranger who has had the

courage to make his permanent home at Davos is Mr. J. A. Symonds, the distinguished art critic and writer on "The Renaissance." *He enjoys fair health, and if one takes into consideration the gravity of his case when he first went to Switzerland, even remarkable health; but if one compares Mr. Symonds physically with the many hale, hearty, broad-shouldered, deep-chested, red-faced giants of strength whom inquiry discovers are men who came here several years ago under supposed sentence of death, one acquires tremendous respect for the curative possibilities of this wonderful climate.

I have written strongly and earnestly because I feel so. If I had known the facts as stated above I would have saved over five years of fruitless wandering in Europe and would to-day be far richer in health and richer in purse. To-day Colorado Springs is comparatively little known, but I venture to prophesy that when physicians and invalids shall have fully tested its wonderful resources in climate and all its other favorable conditions, patients will be crowding to it from all parts of Europe and America, and it will become the great sanatorium of the world for curable cases of consumption.

*Since deceased.

May 10, 1898.

I have just re-read my letter published in 1887, and I cannot see that these eleven years of additional experience with the climate of Colorado Springs have at all changed or modified my opinions. Of course, in the interim, Colorado Springs has grown from a population of seven thousand to twenty-three thousand. The discovery of the marvellous gold camp of Cripple Creek, situated only twenty-five miles from Colorado Springs in an air-line, has greatly added to the wealth and possible development of the city. Cripple Creek has made it decidedly easier to earn a living in Colorado Springs than formerly. The growth of the city, while not detracting from its healthful character owing to the wide spreading-out of its borders, has made possible many improvements which minister to the health, comfort and well-being of its inhabitants. A perfect sewerage system has been introduced; its magnificent pure water supply has been enlarged and greatly improved; and the opportunities of pleasurable enjoyment have been added to many fold. The College and general educational facilities of the community have been developed on a scale which could hardly have been anticipated ten years ago, and altogether Colorado Springs possesses a cluster of climatic, scenic, economic and pleasure advantages, which I believe are nowhere else on this earth combined in such happy proportion. Let me not forget to mention that our hotel and boarding house conditions have grown commensurately with the other advantages of the city, and that invalids can be sure of finding everything desirable in this direction.

As to the bugbear of tubercular infection by bacilli, I find that, so far as Colorado Springs is concerned, it is wholly contradicted by our experience. If consumption developed easily here, it is certain that none would fly from the dangers more speedily and more pertinaciously than families which have already suffered from the dread disease. After nearly thirteen years of life in Colorado Springs, I can say that I do not know of a single instance in the wide range of my acquaintance where tuberculosis has developed owing to infection after arrival here. The theory of such possible infection may, from a medicinal standpoint, be absolutely correct; but it would seem to me that the living experience can be taken as a trustworthy witness against all theory.

The thing which Colorado Springs, in my opinion, urgently needs—and it is almost the only thing—is a large, thoroughly equipped and commodiously-arranged sanatorium. The advantages of such a sanatorium are abundantly shown by the results achieved at such European establishments as the Sanatoria of Falkenstein and Gerbersdorf. Very many young people, especially, come to Colorado Springs, who need the medicinal control and the systematically-planned life which a well-managed sanatorium offers to its patients. This subject has been agitated by some of our prominent physicians, and it is hoped that this want may be satisfactorily supplied at an early date.   LOUIS R. EHRICH.

Vital Statistics.

COLORADO SPRINGS COMPARED WITH STATISTICS OF OTHER CITIES OF SAME POPULATION, BUT OF LOWER ALTITUDE.

By B. B. Grover, M. D., Colorado Springs, Colo.

Having been at the head of the Health Department of this city for the past four years, I have had every opportunity to become familiar with its sanitary condition and I can say without fear of successful contradiction that it is one of the most cleanly cities in the United States.

So many inquiries are being made about its weather and sanitary conditions, that I have thought it would be interesting to present the following comparative tables which speak volumes for our city as an ideal place of residence for the invalid as well as the healthy individual.

The following table shows the total number of deaths in Colorado Springs for the years 1895, 1896 and 1897, also the principal causes of death. It demonstrates at a glance the healthfulness of our people:

Vital Statistics of Colorado Springs. Population averaged for the years 1895, 1896 and 1897, 20,000.

	1895.	1896.	1897.
Total number of deaths	278	355	282
Causes of Death—			
Diphtheria ..	2	13	3
Scarlet Fever	1	8	2
Measles ..	0	3	0
Typhoid Fever	6	20	10
Tuberculosis contracted· elsewhere	130	98	103
Tuberculosis contracted in Colorado	1	2	2
Rheumatism	1	3	1
Heart Disease	15	21	13
Cancer	2	11	9
Diseases of the Digestive System	17	29	24
Diseases of the Respiratory System	21	47	32

Diseases of the Nervous System	32	42	26
Diseases of the Genito-Urinary	12	14	13
Accidental Deaths	7	6	13
All other causes	31	38	31

In the compilation of the data in the following table, I have been careful to select cities from as wide an area as possible, having practically the same population as Colorado Springs, excluding cities in the southern states.

An examination of this table shows but one city, La Crosse, Wis., having a lower death rate than Colorado Springs. Cases of consumption contracted elsewhere should be, and are, excluded in making these comparisons, only cases contracted in the State of Colorado are included.

COMPARATIVE TABLE.

Showing the death rate per 1,000 population of cities of the United States of about the same population as Colorado Springs, but of low altitude:

Average for four years excluding consumption contracted elsewhere.

Colorado Springs	9.10
Adams, Mass	20.62
Alameda, Cal	23.38
Amesbury, Mass.	12.66
Aurora, Ills.	20.32
Cohoes, N. Y.	21.68
Council Bluffs, Ia.	16.44
Danbury, Conn.	20.66
Fresno, Cal.	10.82
Galesburg, Ill.	16.31
La Crosse, Wis.	8.45
Muskegon, Mich.	21.14

Average death rate for the above named cities, 17.50.

Average death rate for all the cities of the United States, having a population of from 15,000 to 25,000, 19.95 per 1,000. Colorado Springs, 9.10.

COMPARATIVE TABLE.

Showing the death rate per 100,000 population in the registration area of the United States and Colorado Springs:

Diseases—	Registration Area of U. S.	Colorado Springs.
Diarrhoeal Diseases	183.71	85.00
Respiratory System Excluding Consumption.	330.30	166.66

Nervous System	247.37	166.66
Circulatory System.	134.22	81.66
Accidents	91.87	43.30
Consumption (a)	245.36	8.33
Malarial Fever	19.19	0
Typhoid Fever	46.27	60.00

a. Contracted in Colorado.

COMPARATIVE TABLE.

Showing the proportion from each cause per 1,000 deaths in the Registration Area of the United States and Colorado Springs:

Diseases—	Registration Area of U. S.	Colorado Springs.
Diarrhoeal Diseases	98.41	75.40
Diseases of Respiratory System, excluding Consumption (a)	160.61	104.00
Diseases of the Nervous System	120.29	108.00
Accidents	51.57	28.50
Circulatory System	65.27	52.45
Rheumatism.	5.36	5.24
Consumption (b)	126.62	3.27
Diphtheria	33.06	19.67
Scarlet Fever	7.10	11.00
Measles	11.00	3.27
Malarial Fever.	22.10	0
Typhoid Fever	32.16	39.34

a. This rate would be reduced to 64.00 if cases of consumption, in which the immediate cause of death was pneumonia, were excluded.

b. Contracted in Colorado.

The following table of meteorological data compiled by Mr. P. E. Doudna, observer at Colorado College, in this city, shows the temperature, humidity, sunshine and rainfall of Colorado Springs for the past twenty-five years:

SUMMARY: METEOROLOGICAL DATA FOR COLORADO SPRINGS, 1871 TO 1897.

MONTHLY AVERAGE.

	Jan.	Feb.	March	April	May	June	July	Aug.	Sept.	Oct.	Nov.	Dec.
Mean temperature	27	31	37	45	54	63	69	67	59	48	36	31
Lowest temperature	13	16	23	32	41	49	55	54	45	35	24	18
Highest temperature	42	44	50	59	68	78	84	80	73	63	49	44
Mean rel. humidity	53	59	53	50	50	49	52	55	50	49	53	55
Total monthly precipitation in inches	0.16	0.29	0.57	1.35	2.48	1.36	3.14	2.26	1.04	0.62	0 31	0 26
Clear days	17	13	13	12	11	13	11	12	17	21	19	18
Cloudy days	4	4	6	6	8	5	5	5	4	4	3	5
Partly cloudy days.	10	11	12	12	12	12	15	14	9	6	8	8

Total rainfall, 1897, 11.62 inches.

Average rainfall for sixteen years, 14.46 inches.

CITY WATER SUPPLY.

The water used for domestic purposes by the city comes from the snow-capped mountain, Pike's Peak, above any point of possible contamination. The water is piped from Lake Moraine direct into each residence of the city. The water from melting snow is collected in reservoirs as follows:

Reservoir No. 7, area, 40 acres, elevation 12,200 feet.

Reservoir No. 8, area, 140 acres, elevation 11,800 feet.

Reservoir No. 2, area, 40 acres, elevation 11,300 feet.

Lake Moraine, area, 100 acres, elevation 10,278 feet.

The weekly bacteriological examination of the city water shows the highest number of colonies per c. c., to be 110 and the lowest 48.

Standards for filtered water: Below 100 colonies per c. c., good; between 100 and 200 suspicious, but usable; above 200 bad.

The Manitou Springs.

BUT FIVE MILES DISTANT FROM COLORADO SPRINGS AND CONNECTED BY THREE CAR LINES.

The celebrated mineral springs were held in awe and adoration by the Indians in prehistoric days, for these waters cured their ills and their potency was ascribed to Divinity. Hence the springs were called "Manitou"—The Great Spirit. The developed springs, "Manitou," "Navajo," &c., form, probably, the largest Soda Springs in the world. Strongly impregnated with natural carbonic acid gas, all the springs of the group are powerfully effervescent. The many forms of dyspepsia and stomach troubles are peculiarly susceptible to this water's salutary influences. Its assimilating powers are remarkable and it is an excellent appetizer, exhilarating and refreshing.

The analysis of the principal springs by Profesor Elwyn-Waller, Ph. D., Analytical Chemist, Columbia College, New York City, are as follows:

ANALYSIS OF MANITOU SODA SPRINGS.

GRAINS PER PINT:			
	MANITOU.	NAVAJO.	UTE.
Sodium Chloride	2.993	2.974	2.116
Potassium Sulphate	1.336	1.244	0.979
Sodium "	1 268	1.367	1.880
Sodium Bicarbonate	8.056	8.442	5.725
Lithium "	0.162	0.142	0.025
Calcium "	13.989	14.041	6.421
Magnesium "	3.624	3.486	1.747
Iron Oxide	0.003	0.003	0.076
Alumina	0.009	0.013	0 019
Silica	0.312	0.308	0.452
TOTALS.	31.752	32.020	19.440

Manitou Park.

In the Mountains, between Denver and Colorado Springs.

The so-called "Parks" of the Rocky Mountains are often referred to, and deserve the special attention of the medical profession. Between the ranges are found numerous open spaces—parts of the plateau which have not been upheaved. These open spaces are clothed with fine grass, from which noble spruce and pine trees rise majestically, either singly or in groups, presenting the appearance more of a well kept park than of any other familiar form of landscape; and thus "Park" has become the local name now generally applied to these open spaces. They are usually very beautiful, calm and peaceful, and possess a brilliancy of atmosphere and an invigorating purity in the air which cannot be surpassed. They are invariably surrounded by pine forests.

Disregarding the four great "Parks", which occupy the summit of the plateau, and are wide plains, not particularly attractive, and too elevated, we find some especially beautiful parks of smaller size, lying between the Rampart Range, or Eastern Foot Hills, and the snow-capped mountains themselves. North of Denver, Estes Park is the finest; South of Denver, Manitou Park is the most attractive, and possesses advantages which, if more generally known, would be greatly appreciated.

Manitou Park is easily reached and is very beautiful. Here those who delight in the invigorating pleasures of this mountain region, as well as the delicate who are seeking health and need repose and dry air, will have their wishes fulfilled. The Park has been the private property of Dr. W. A. Bell, (formerly a London physician, but no longer in practice), for over twenty-five years, and he has devoted much thought, money and time to the erection and good management of an Hotel Establishment, which meets the more exacting requirements of such as are acquainted with the comforts of the resorts of Switzerland, and are now "exploring" the Rocky Mountain region.

Particulars of the hotel accommodations are to be found on another page. What we especially desire to point out here is that this property, consisting of between 9,000 and 10,000 acres, being nine miles long by two miles wide, has been appropriated to the pursuit of health and recreation. For sanatorium purposes there are to be found within the Park spots which fill all the conditions most to be desired. The elevation averages 7,700 feet above sea level, corresponding as to temperature to about 4,500 feet in Switzerland, at which elevation the most successful health resorts are to be found. The soil is a disintegrated granite, very porous and dry; the air is fragrant with the odor of the pines.

The medical profession has become convinced by experience that it is at establishments especially equipped for the purpose, and situated in a dry and elevated mountainous region, that the best results in the treatment of tuberculosis are obtained. Already there are over one hundred such establishments in the Alps. It is high time that we, having at our doors a climate infinitely superior to that of Switzerland from a hygienic point of view, should follow the lead of those eminent European physicians who have evolved the new system of treatment which has proved so marvellously successful.

THE MANITOU PARK HOTEL ESTABLISHMENT.

The Manitou Park Hotel Establishment consists of a hotel, having the general character of an eastern country club, and several cottages of various sizes from sixteen to five rooms each, tributary to it; all well built, and all furnished and kept up on a scale of excellence which as yet is unusual in the Rocky Mountains. There is accommodation for 150 visitors, who have the choice of occupying cottages apart, or of living in the hotel.

Golf, lawn tennis, croquet, riding, driving, boating, trout fishing, bicycling and music are the chief amusements.

HOW TO REACH MANITOU PARK.

The Park is situated fifteen miles by road west of Palmer Lake, on the west side of the Rampart Range. It is eight miles north of Woodland Station, on the Colorado Midland Railway. Woodland Station is fifteen miles above Manitou, in the Ute Pass, and is on a through route to California. Coaches for Manitou Park leave Palmer Lake on the arrival of the morning Denver trains over the D. & R. G. and A. T. & S. F. Railways, reaching the Park Hotel in time for luncheon. There is also a daily stage from Woodland Station, and carriages from the Park livery can be ordered by telegraph to Woodland Station, where there is a telephone to the Manitou Park Hotel.

For particulars apply to Messrs. Neilson & McLachlan, Manitou Park Hotel, Torrington, Colo.

Telegrams to Woodland Park.